Eighteen Brothers and Sisters,

a memoir by Seeta Begui

Eighteen Brothers and Sisters,

a memoir by Seeta Begui

Seeta Media, Inc.
Satellite Beach, Florida 32937
2012

TITLE: *Eighteen Brothers and Sisters, a memoir by Seeta Begui*
AUTHOR: Seeta Begui (December 30, 1963 -   )
PRINT EDITION ISBN-13: 9781467910415
NUMBER OF PAGES PRINT EDITION: 241 pages

BISAC Categories
BIO 022000   BIOGRAPHY & AUTOBIOGRAPHY / Women
FAM 001030 FAMILY & RELATIONSHIPS / Abuse / Domestic Partner Abuse
FAM 016000   FAMILY & RELATIONSHIPS / Education
SOC 002010   CONTEMPORARY CULTURAL ANTHROPOLOGY

LCCN: 2012901777

FIRST EDITION
THIRD PRINTING: 5   7   9   10   8   6   4
RELEASE DATE: April 2012
PUBLISHER CONTACT INFORMATION:
Seeta Media, Inc.,
Satellite Beach, FL 32937
Seetamedia@aol.com
www.Seetamedia.com

DOLR: 20120319-1724

Preface

The book *Eighteen Brothers and Sisters, a memoir by Seeta Begui* is an inspirational message of the power of sacrifices, mentors, education and training to make a difference. The book chronicles Seeta's upbringing, her struggles to become educated, and her accomplishments achieved by her determination and thanks to the teamwork of her phenomenal extended family and the angels in the right place at the right time to guide her.

As the story unfolds, the voice, attitude, and intonation reflect the age Seeta was at the time. The voice changes as she transforms from a straggly three-year-old to the beautiful, accomplished woman of influence and means she has become today.

Methodology: To prepare this book, Seeta interviewed family members. Several names were changed to protect their identities and reputations.

Geography: Trinidad is the most southern island in the Caribbean, and bordered on the North by the Caribbean Sea, and on the East by the Atlantic Ocean. Separated by the Columbus Channel, seven miles south-southwest of Trinidad is the coastline of Venezuela and west of Trinidad is the Gulf of Paria.

Introduction

After the abolition of slavery in Trinidad and Tobago in 1836, most African slaves felt that they were mentally freed from the sugarcane plantations. However, the British landowners still required laborers. The price of sugar was high in the world economy, so the British turned to India for substitute slave labor.

The history of Trinidad and Tobago and the arrival of Indian immigrants from India also represents our family's history.

Indian immigrants came from India to make a new home in the country of Trinidad and Tobago, but entered as a social minority into a social-and-political environment where the British controlled the majority race, the Africans. Some viewed the Indian minority as "coming to take jobs."

Our family's forefathers immigrated into that kind of setting.

For Indian immigrants, it also meant that the cultural-and-religious traditions from India were more strictly enforced in Trinidad and Tobago than in India, because while India is a sprawling, vast, ever changing, complex, complicated country, Trinidad and Tobago are a very small islands. Indians in this new land held onto their customs more rigorously than they would have in India itself. What that meant, and its relevance for our family was, it was unheard of for a woman to be "on the side" or a mistress, because Indian culture is one where a man has only one wife and family. A number of factors created the situation where my mother became my father's mistress. Dhoon Ramlogan was already legally married to his wife Jaya. This was a time when communication was limited to mail by ground transportation. Motor cars were a rarity, and communication was difficult. It was easier to keep a secret.

Seeta's granddaughter Madison.

Dedication
My Reflection

I wrote this book, a story of our strengths, struggles, challenges, initiatives, hardwork, and, for the most part, fortunate endings, for you my children and grandchildren, so you might know about your parents, grandparents and great grandparents, and all that we survived.

I wrote it to let you know what strong people you come from and the sacrifices that were made. This way, you will know that you, too, can be such a blessing. I want you to know your roots so you know why to value education, hardwork, family, and making good decisions. I want you to realize your own inner strengths so you will find a way to accomplish your highest dreams.

Seeta Begui

Content

Chapter 1: Under the Lemon Tree in Corial

In 1966, when I was three, I looked up to my big brother Mike, who was four. We began each day relatively clean, but dirt poor. Mother made sure Mike and I were reasonably clean when she left home in the morning.

We lived in the village of Corial in the recently-formed Republic of Trinidad and Tobago. Our mother Rajdaye was a housemaid, a laundress, and cleaning lady. In the harvest seasons, she cut sugarcane to earn a living.

Each weekday we were told, "Seeta and Mike, sit under the little lemon tree at the far end of the yard. Be good because your mother has to work. Stay put under the tree."

Corial is where I was born and lived with mother and my siblings until I was seven. The village was alive in the mornings with people talking, laughing and walking. Alive with life!

We could easily hear people outside brushing their teeth, spitting, snorting, and coughing – as normal daily village life. Mike and I noticed things like that because we didn't own a real toothbrush. Our mother selected certain species of shrubbery and broke off twigs. We each chewed a twig to fray the end into bristles to brush our teeth.

In those days, anything we needed to do in the village meant taking a walk. In the morning, I enjoyed being with my mother and Mike, walking to the other end of Corial where we filled containers with water to bring home.

An ebb and flow of people walking together moved in the mornings. For example, villagers walked to get water at five a.m. Most ladies brought laundry to wash at the pond, spring, or creek. There was a constant banter of conversations.

It was interesting for Mike and me. We had a nice feeling when people were doing things together. In the early morning group, we felt as if we belonged. But the truth was Mike and I didn't really belong. For those few minutes each morning, we pretended.

Because of the gossip about our family, to me Corial was not a loving place.

By that time, mother only had a small family of six children. On these outings, she generally spoke only to ladies whom she trusted.

Unfortunately, a lot of those ladies knew my father was not just charming and good-looking, but he was a womanizer. Needless to say, that didn't stop me from loving him.

Two or three women in particular had taken up mother's cause and had spoken to the rest of the village on her behalf. They defended mother explaining it was not my mother's fault that she was "associated with" my father and had "those other children."

Mother purchased piglets and made them a pen at the edge of our property. Although Hindu people are not supposed to eat pork, it was well known that these piglets were being fattened. One would become our Christmas dinner, and the other two were to be sold allowing the proceeds to buy necessities and, hopefully, even Christmas presents.

Kuchi was our favorite of the piglets being saved for Christmas. It was our job to make sure the three little pigs had access to water all day long. Every two hours or so, we ran down the hill to the little pig pen to check on them. Then we ran back to the lemon tree.

No matter how clean we tried to keep the piglets, pigs will be pigs, and sometimes they were very dirty. It could not be helped, but sometimes we also smelled like pigs. When Mike and I were under our lemon tree, using it as a bathroom, as a place to sit, as a place of refuge, even bare footed, with our hair all matted and bodies smelling of hogs, we still believed we were clean kids because our mother had shined us up with oil in the morning before she left for work.

We waited under the tree until mother's one o'clock lunch break when she checked on us and brought us some rice. Then, she returned to wherever she was working.

After she left, Kuchi ate scraps, whatever we had left.

It didn't matter that our house had no air conditioning, indoor plumbing, or electricity, because we sat outside at the edge of our property under the tree. We were still living with our mother – something, at that time, our four older siblings could not do. Therefore, we felt it was some kind of a privilege. That tree was our security then.

In the meantime, pedestrians passed by along the street. It was never dull. We liked to people-watch.

We felt safe by that lemon tree. The typical Corial village life to me was kind of fun because we didn't know any difference. When you're poor, it isn't so bad if you don't know you are poor. Not until we went to school, did we find out just how poor we were.

We were well-behaved kids. We never left. When we sat under the lemon tree or tended Kuchi and the other piglets, we were outside all day. Our paternal grandparents lived directly across the street, but we were not allowed to go there. Their house was built into a hillside on large bamboo poles for support. We thought they looked like stilts. Under the shaded front of their house was a shady lanai, a room with three walls that was open at the front.

The lanai had two hammocks and a settee (a homemade backless bench). Coconut fiber was stuffed into flour sacks to make cushions for the settee. Most houses had at least one. Grandmother Ramlogan's settee was especially nice. It was pushed against a wall to give back support. We yearned to sit on it and be near to them, but our grandparents didn't allow us come over to share the shade under their house.

The Ramlogan grandparents had their own kids and other grandchildren living in their extended household or on the property. These grandparents also worked cutting sugarcane, as a result they were in and out of their house during the day.

While under the tiny tree, Mike and I watched them from afar. We'd watch for Grandfather Baap to sit with

Grandmother Moya and take mid-afternoon naps in the lanai before going back to the sugarcane fields.

After months of pig sitting, one morning after mother put us under the lemon tree, we looked down the hillside and didn't see any pigs in our pen. We ran down the hill to check. The gate to the pen was wide open, and the pigs were gone. Kuchi was gone. So was our Christmas dinner and along with any hope of receiving shoes, or any Christmas present.

When we children played, it was most often outdoors. For this reason, when the neighbors spoke of Dhoon Ramlogan's "outside children," we thought that's what it meant. We didn't learn until later that the remarks were derogatory.

PART I THE VILLAGE OF GASPARILLO

Chapter 2: Mother's First Marriage

To understand our family now and when I was growing up, it is important to know what life was like for our mother before we came along. As was the Hindu custom, when my mother Rajdaye Balkissoon came of age in 1950 at 15, her parents arranged for her to marry Ram Harri. Ram was a charming man, but not wealthy, who enjoyed Hindi music and cutting cane. It was a first marriage for both.

After the wedding, Rajdaye moved in with Ram in his parent's household. As a new bride, Rajdaye found married life difficult because of the expectations of her in-laws and the unending number of chores they assigned to her. Ram continued to enjoy the sporting life: gambling, and drinking. He failed to assume the prescribed life stage, duties, and responsibilities to Raj of her husband.

Rajdaye sought her parents' support by formally requesting a family meeting at their house in Gasparillo. She walked there and told her father, "It is very sad, but my marriage isn't working out. Ram is a big spender with nothing left to take care of me. His parents treat me lower than a slave. I don't have any children as yet, so I want a divorce or an annulment, now."

Her father Sookai Balkissoon refused. "Rajdaye, you will do no such thing. In our culture, you stay put! You must remain in the marriage arranged for you. Be a good wife to your husband. You cannot stay with us. You must return to him, because that's where you live, child. It's your home."

"Father, you don't understand," Rajdaye said. "In that household and in my marriage, my life is no better than that of a servant. While my husband loafs or is out gallivanting, I must slave to care for his parents and their home as well as be outside cutting sugarcane in the scorching sun — working like a man among the men. You know that isn't right."

"This is your lot. Go home," Sookai ordered.

Reluctantly, obediently, she returned to her in-laws' household.

What her father Sookai didn't tell Rajdaye was that he had failed to fulfill his parental obligation. Before consenting to the match, he was supposed to check out her prospective husband and his family diligently. As a family, he and his brothers should have visited the Harri's family clan to check the young man's family history, his job, his personal habits, his prospects to be a loving husband and a good provider. Sookai and his brothers were responsible to be sure the men and women in the prospect's family were of good character and impeccable reputation. All this was supposed to have happened before he agreed to the arranged marriage for her.

Instead, in a late-night poker game where the rum flowed freely, when he found himself cash short, Sookai Balkissoon wagered his daughter's hand in marriage and lost. Ram Harri's father won. Since he was already married, he awarded Rajdaye to his son Ram. With a deal of the cards, the arranged marriage sealed Rajdaye to young Ram Harri.

Sookai was not only a gambler, he was also a heavy drinker.

This marriage with Ram was saturated with verbal abuse and domestic violence. Rajdaye learned of the card game after she was married. She conceived two children with him prior to their divorce.

❧🌸❧

The family still maintained the Indian culture and traditions, where a woman is "meant to be subservient." With limited opportunities in a society as a woman and as a social minority, a woman needed the protection of a man.

A woman became someone to be looked after, but not always as property. Some men treated a wife with respect, and Some men genuinely loved the woman to whom they were married.

The prevalent thinking in the male-oriented society, then and somewhat now, was that if a man got a woman pregnant, he snuffed any possibility she might have of an alternative life or future with anyone else. She was basically now his property. A pregnancy was like a deed, a manifestation of his property right. It was like putting up a flag in front of her that said, "This is mine."

ະ❧ະ

Even while nursing an infant, Rajdaye was still expected to clean the house, prepare the food, cut sugarcane, wait on her husband and his parents and any extended family members who decided to stay there or drop by.

Within a year, Rajdaye returned to her parents and told them emphatically that this marriage was not working. She explained how bad her situation was with her husband who refused to work, and her father again urged her to go home to her husband.

In desperation, instead of going home, Rajdaye jumped into the river intending to drown, but it was the dry season, and the water was too shallow.

Knowing she couldn't swim, her younger brothers and sisters ran to tell Sookai that Rajdaye was drowning. By the time they got back to help her, a man had offered her one end of a stick and pulled her out.

Because of this attempt, her father knew for certain her marital situation was dire. He felt guilty that he had caused her to be in this situation. Had Rajdaye's father been willing to take her back the first time, the story would have had an entirely different outcome.

Instead of sending her away, Sookai suggested another solution. "Rajdaye, I have a little plot of land behind this house. Perhaps I could build a small house there for you and the children."

This time, her father gave her a small plot of land and they built a shell of a 10-x10-foot house. Rajdaye completed the construction by chinking between the boards to keep the wind and rain out. The style of construction is what we called "a board house."

Chapter 3: Our Maternal Ancestors

After hearing my mother's story, I wondered what her mother and grandmother were like. Were they also strong women?

Born on the British-ruled island of Trinidad, my Grandmother Kasey was fair and beautiful, the daughter of a green-eyed Scot woman who married a man called 'Coalpot' Ablack (pronounced *Ab-lack*) who was from Bihar, India. My Great-grandfather Ablack married outside his Hindu religion, and the marriage was not an arranged one. His wife was probably Presbyterian. Nevertheless, their children were reared in the strict Hindu culture and religion.

While degree of skin color was made a big issue within our Indian culture, his nickname 'Coalpot' came about not due to skin tone – as he was of a light complexion – but because he preferred to roast corn, eggplant, and tomatoes outside on a grate above a coal-fired cooking pot. Thus, most conversations with him were said to be "over the coalpot." Coalpot lived past 75 years of age.

Some say his wife died in childbirth; others said she returned to Scotland.

Their daughter, Kasey Ablack, my grandmother, met and married Sookai Balkissoon in Trinidad. The couple made their home in the village of Gasparillo near Goodman Trace. Sookai Balkissoon and Kasey Ablack's first-born was a daughter named Rajdaye born in 1935. She was the eldest of their 12 children.

What I remember most of my Grandmother Kasey Balkissoon was her resourcefulness and independence. She thought for herself. She passed that heritage to her daughter Rajdaye, and I am grateful my grandmother and mother both passed those traits to me.

Because both of Rajdaye's parents worked outside of the home, as their children grew, most of the family's childcare duties fell to Rajdaye.

In seeking to learn more about our mother, my family and I wanted to understand how Rajdaye developed so much emotional strength.

My mother's sister, my Aunt Angela told a story about a day their parents Sookai and Kasey Balkissoon went to work far from the house, and didn't return until dark. "We kids were left at home all day with nothing to eat," Angela said. "My eldest sister Rajdaye was also just a young girl, but she fended to find food for her siblings. We lived without electricity or running water. We were without food and hungry kids. I'll never forget what Rajdaye did. She grabbed a rock and a knife, jumped our neighbor's fence, and hurled the rock at their snarling watchdog to make him back off long enough for her to cut a stalk of green bananas. She tossed the heavy stick of bananas to our side of the fence and climbed back over the fence. She built a fire, boiled the bananas in salted water, and gave them to us to eat. When one brother asked for more, she gave him her own portion . . . Rajdaye was especially pretty with curly hair, her mother's green eyes, and a light tan complexion. Her good looks complicated her life."

With more than 12 children to support, that family had hardships and challenges.

Sugarcane was the main cash crop of the island. The British offered ownership of sugarcane land as an incentive to immigrate. Sookai acquired sugarcane land and other property. This was a step up socially.

My mother, Rajdaye, stayed in Gasparillo with her two children, and also helped her parents with their 11 other children. Although my mother now had two children, she was still an extremely beautiful 25-year-old woman.

While mother lacked education and was functionally-illiterate, she was smart and desirable. She knew how to manage money with limited resources. In addition, Rajdaye hired out as a laundress doing washing and ironing, cooking, and cutting sugarcane.

After she left Ram Harri, her father helped her apply for an annulment. When that failed, they started the process for a divorce.

For a man to apply for a divorce or annulment generally took eight months; but it was unheard of and a scandal for a woman to apply for an annulment or divorce in her own right. In the Indian community, it became the talk of the town.

When the divorce proceedings began, Rajdaye adjusted to being a single working mother. She was not seeking another man, nor was she involved with anyone. She just wanted to be totally released from her obligations to Ram and the Harri family.

As most divorced or separated women soon learn when there are children in the marriage, the adults are never truly free of one another. While living with their mother, their children often stayed with their father and his family.

Villagers didn't use court-ordered visitation schedules to make arrangements. However, without a formal schedule, it could be stressful on parents and children alike.

Each time their father took care of the kids, Rajdaye worked in the sugarcane fields or other menial jobs. With limited education, there were not many paying jobs available to her to support herself and her children.

Three generations: Kimberly Durjan, Seeta
Ramlogan Begui, and Rajdaye Balkissoon.

Chapter 4: Deen & Raj

When she secured a position as a domestic servant in the well-to-do Rahim family, it seemed a wonderful blessing. His family were shopkeepers. However, her parents and members of the community frowned upon a Hindu woman being in the employ of a Muslim family. Rajdaye knew she had to be practical. The wages were better, and the employment was not seasonal. The position was to be year-around in their home. She was a good employee, and the Rahim family gave her increasingly responsible work.

Their son Deen noticed the beautiful young Rajdaye and was soon smitten with her. He created opportunities to speak to her, to see her each day, and soon fell in love.

Rajdaye liked Deen, too. There was an unmistakable chemistry between them. This was her first experience with the feeling of 'being in love.'

It was the same way for him. When Deen asked her to marry him, Rajdaye had to explain her awkward legal circumstance, that she had been married and her divorce was pending. Deen promised to marry her as soon as her divorce became final. In the meantime, the couple kept their love a secret. She pressed the court for a decision, but the court issued one postponement after another.

The intensity of feelings between Deen and Rajdaye grew and could no longer be denied. They experienced a bliss neither had known could exist. But they were also uninformed about birth control, and soon Rajdaye gave birth to Sarah, who was called "Dolly."

When Deen's daughter Sarah was born, the Gasparillo villagers assumed Rajdaye was having the child with her estranged husband. Nobody really knew about the affair except Rajdaye and Deen. Since Rajdaye was still technically a married woman, and the Rahim elders didn't yet know of her divorce petition, it was presumed she was still having relations with her legal husband Ram.

Deen and Rajdaye didn't set the record straight.

The court continued to delay not wanting to set a precedent of granting a divorce initiated by and on behalf of a woman.

Soon Rajdaye was pregnant with Deen's second love child. The following January, their daughter Molly was born. This time, the baby looked like Deen's baby pictures, and their first daughter's facial features grew more like Deen's side of the family.

His parents became suspicious. When the couple was found out, Deen petitioned his parents to ask for their blessings to marry Rajdaye.

The Rahim family was horrified. They refused because she was a married Hindu woman with two children in wedlock and now two illegitimate daughters of mixed parentage. Rajdaye was a woman who was so brazen as to petition the court for a divorce on her own. What would she do to Deen after they were married?

Deen loved her deeply and insisted he wanted to marry her. The Rahim family was furious. In their culture, the worst thing a woman could do was to have children and then fall in love with someone who did not. Although it had not bothered them before, they played the religion card. Because she was Hindu and they were Muslim, they refused to approve a marriage between Deen and Rajdaye.

In both the Indian and Muslim cultures, a divorced or separated woman with two out-of-wedlock children, was viewed as dishonorable, and the Rahim family let her know it. Deen's parents broke up the couple's relationship and fired Rajdaye, wanting nothing more to do with her or the two illegitimate children. Rajdaye was ordered off the property, and the Rahim family disowned the children of their union.

Rajdaye was in love with a man of a different faith who was forbidden to have contact with her. He knew if he stayed with Rajdaye, his parents would cut him off financially. While waiting for her divorce to be finalized, she gave birth to Deen's two illegitimate children. Her reputation in the village was in a shambles and her secure year-round housekeeping job was lost.

Yet she and Deen still loved each other, and this added to the pain of their separation and heartbreak.

Deen was a good man who loved his daughters and at first wanted to raise them. His parents finally agreed that he could provide for them and raise them, but only if Rajdaye was completely out of the picture. The children were not to be exposed to Hinduism but raised exclusively in the Muslim faith.

For Rajdaye to agree to these terms, and have Dolly and Molly raised in the Muslim faith, would alienate Rajdaye's parents.

In Gasparillo, there were few secrets, but many assumptions. In those days, while Hindu and Muslim villagers chatted, they went to different places of worship. The buzz in the village among the Indian Hindu faction was that Rajdaye had continued to see her husband even after they had separated. "How else could she have four children in four years!" Most Hindu people had not heard of her liaison with the Muslim Rahim family's favorite son, Deen. Rajdaye didn't set them straight.

Regardless of her parent's attitudes, in her community, because of her beauty and personality, Rajdaye could do little wrong. Most villagers assumed all four kids were from her first husband.

Sookai loved Rajdaye and all his children. He told each daughter she was his prettiest daughter, but to Rajdaye, her beauty had become her curse. Now there were five people living in a small hut behind his home, which the family called Number 10. Nevertheless, her father said, "Rajdaye, we've tried to help you, but you have to find a way to provide for your own children."

Rajdaye was in a difficult situation economically, socially, and physically. What was she going to do? She could cook, clean, and sew.

She realized it was essential to secure another position to have any hope of solving her problems in the long run. She must bring in income in any respectable way she could. With four children all under four, she did what she had to do—she went back to being a laundress doing washing and ironing. In season, she picked up her machete to become a full-time field hand, cutting sugarcane in the fields of other local families.

Rajdaye was very sad. Doing manual labor in the hot sun, her heart ached for Deen. She had her hands full taking care of four small children – two still in cloth diapers and nursing.

In her humiliation, desperation, and poverty, Rajdaye went to see her first husband's family to ask for child support for the first two children.

After she was fired, news soon came that Deen was being sent away to study. Her dreams of a possible reunion were crushed once again when she found out her beloved Deen was being coerced into an arranged marriage to a Muslim girl with a more appropriate status for him.

Rajdaye found out where and when the marriage was to take place and that day, she went to a neighbor's house with a rooftop view of the ceremony. The rooftop was a place where Rajdaye and her sisters had frequently gathered mangoes that fell onto the nearly flat roof. She had a clear view of the courtyard across the street where the ceremony was taking place. Deen, her true love, friend, and father of two of her children was marrying someone else. She wept quietly as she watched him forever slip away from her. Her hopes of happily-ever-after were permanently dashed. This broke her heart.

After this painful transition was made, back at Number 10, she still had to support Molly and Sarah ("Dolly"). When sugarcane-cutting season ended, Rajdaye got a job sweeping the floors in a large elementary school building and her divorce was also finalized.

Chapter 5: *Kismet* in the Courtyard

Our father later told us, "I was driving in town down a narrow street in heavy traffic, so my car was barely moving. When I glanced toward the elementary school, I noticed an incredibly beautiful woman sweeping the front courtyard. I felt an overwhelming urge to find out who she was. As fate would have it, there was an available parking space in front of the school."

Dhoon's friends often described him as having "a long eye for a pretty woman." Dhoon was a relatively tall Indian man. He was well-built and cut a handsome authoritative and intelligent picture. He was a confident man who knew how to engage a lady in conversation. It was perhaps this charm and charismatic appeal that made him so attractive to women of all races.

ॐ❧ॐ

Our mother Rajdaye told us her version. "I had a new job as a janitor at an elementary school. One morning in 1960, while I was sweeping the front courtyard at the elementary school, a gentleman parked his car, and came into the schoolyard. He cut a dashing figure in his police uniform! A handsome but dark-complected Indian man." Rajdaye continued, "It would cause trouble with my parents, especially since I already had four children to support – two children from Mr. Ram and two from Mr. Deen – two Hindu children and two Muslim children. I knew better than to become

22

involved with another man. But, this was fate."

As he came closer, she didn't dare look up. *The last thing I needed was to attract the attention of another man,* she thought.

In the courtyard, he approached her and made conversation. Rajdaye was polite but claimed she wasn't really interested in him. She was thinking, *With four kids in four years, I don't need any more trouble. . . . But he really has a nice car.*

Back in those days, people thought that if a man had a car and had land, he was a somebody.

The next day, Rajdaye went about her duties, but her mind returned often to thoughts about the good-looking man in a uniform who had his own car.

After that day, the man made it a point to come to the school every few days, and each time, he sought out Rajdaye.

His attention began to wear through her resistance. Wearing a uniform and having a nice car made her think he might be a good catch, but she still didn't want to be interested in him. She had her hands full working to raise her four children.

Rajdaye had to look out for her future and that of the children, just as any other mother would. By now, she had also established a pattern of being a risk-taker and breaking the societal rules and traditions of our Indian and Hindu culture. In this sense, mother was a liberated woman for that time and dared to break some important rules of the society. She was also a leader in our country when women were not to discuss politics.

The next time the uniformed policeman had business at the school, before leaving, he made conversation and told her his name was Dhoon Ramlogan.

Secretly, this time Rajdaye later told us that she felt like a liberated woman to be talking with a man in public. However, she wasn't liberated enough to ask if he had a wife or any children, or why he was making frequent trips to come to an elementary school.

One day when her shift was over, Dhoon offered to give her a ride home. That night, at the main house she even dared to mention the policeman to her father.

"I'll do some checking," her father replied. "This man likes you, you know. I can tell." Sookai said, "Now I've seen his car! Some rig! He has a car . . . Has such an important job that he wears a uniform. He stands tall and he wears shiny shoes." He nodded his head in an approving way.

Material things so easily fooled the family! A car, a uniform, a man standing tall and wearing shiny shoes.

A few days later when Rajdaye came home from work, her father gestured for her to sit with him. "Rajdaye, perhaps you should invite him home one night — so I can take a closer look."

When Dhoon came home to meet her parents, Sookai seemed happy. Later, he said he thought, *Well, maybe she's going to get somebody to actually marry her, and take care of her and all four children. I can have my backyard back.*

ঌঌ❦ঌঌ

In the Indian Hindu culture, a grown-up daughter has to have a man. A woman should never live by herself. The economy was not set up to allow a woman to find a job sufficient to sustain herself and her children. Their cultural norm was a man takes care of a woman and supports his children; and that's that. But mother was a risk-taker; she broke many norms of our society.

All during the time Rajdaye was on her own working at the school, she also had to arrange child care, visitation, be a parent, and deal with the strife between sets of grandparents — the Rahim family and the Harri family. Deen's new wife did not welcome his illegitimate daughters. The grandparents of Molly and Dolly wanted full custody of the little girls so they could be raised Muslim without taint of Rajdaye's reputation and exposure to Hindu culture. Deen family's scorn also made his children feel like 'outside children.'

Whenever Rajdaye tried to put Deen out of her mind, other thoughts, such as the painful fear of losing these children intruded. When they went to visit, she worried. She wanted to keep the family together. Just the thought that she might not have her children under her roof was enough to cause stabbing pains of angst.

She did her best at least to keep these youngest of her

children living at home. Deen's two daughters occasionally spent time with him and his parents. These children only really felt loved with their mother.

☙ ❦ ☙

Later Raj told me she still yearned for Deen, even when she started seeing Dhoon socially. Little did she know that this man would become her ultimate partner for the rest of her life.

Whenever her father brought up the subject of making arrangements for a proper arranged marriage, Dhoon deftly avoided setting a date or agreeing to any specifics. So, instead of the wedding Sookai had anticipated for his daughter, he again failed to investigate with sufficient due diligence.

Eventually, Rajdaye found herself pregnant by Dhoon, the man of few words and at least six secrets already.

In the early 1960s, birth control methods had not been perfected and the pill, considered to be experimental medicine, was not generally available, even to well-to-do women. A poor woman in a developing country had no access to the dependable birth control products that are available now.

When Rajdaye and Dhoon had a son in 1962, he was given the name Mike. At that time, Mike was not given his father's surname, Ramlogan.

The next year, 1963, Rajdaye was pregnant with me. I was the first daughter of Rajdaye and Dhoon Ramlogan. They named me Seeta. In the Hindu religion, Seeta was the misunderstood and maligned wife of a Prince who later became King.

Since I was an illegitimate child, I was given my mother's maiden name as my surname and I was known by that surname until I was 11 years of age.

Chapter 6: National Independence

When the British rulers left in 1962, two islands joined to become the Republic of Trinidad and Tobago, and the new country became an independent member of the British Commonwealth. A new currency was commissioned, called "Trinidad and Tobago dollars" or "TT-dollars," to make the distinction from "US-dollars" or "USD."

This bloodless transition left a power vacuum which resulted in a great deal of political turmoil and social upheaval as the nation's ethnic communities (East Indian, Black, Chinese, White, Middle Eastern as well as indigenous Carib, Arawak, and others) sought to improve their standard of living and create a better life for their families.

Land represented wealth. A person owning land was considered to be well off. People who were wise saw their future with land and bought as much as they could. Ownership and occupancy of land was a place to belong, to live, to grow food for sustenance or to sell, but also a commodity that could be sold or leveraged for a better life.

Under the British rule, when the authorities divided up the land parcels to reallocate them, my extended family received more land. Father's family, the Ramlogans, bought sugarcane land that others did not want. This was very fortunate. They had land to give mother when she needed it most.

ﻩﺎﻩﺎ

Although they were far away from the ancestral homeland, these East Indian immigrants felt emotionally attached to it. All the traditional problems of the fighting between India-Pakistan continued that feud in the Caribbean. Culturally, in Trinidad, most Muslims and Hindus tried to get along.

Chapter 7: Dhoon's Duplicity Became Public

During this transition and upheaval in Trinidad and Tobago, all hell broke loose in Gasparillo and in our family.

Someone of importance came to Sookai's front door and was invited inside.

"That man, Mr. Dhoon Ramlogan, who has been coming around to see your most beautiful daughter, is actually a married man with a wife and at least six children in Corial!"

By the time Rajdaye found out, it was too late.

Sookai didn't confront Dhoon, but took it out on Rajdaye. He angrily gave his daughter an ultimatum. "You have to leave. You have shamed us. We are very disappointed. You have brought nothing but shame and destruction to this family. Now that all this is public knowledge, we have no choice. We've tried to help you, but this is too much. You can no longer be under my roof or live on my property. You have to find another place to live and another way to provide for all six of your children. You must leave at once!"

This was also an embarrassment and a losing of face for him because he had again failed to check out a prospective suitor for his daughter.

"You've done it again. Another set of kids with another

man. You are setting a bad example for your sisters and brothers living at home."

She tearfully begged him for more time.

Apparently, because Sookai liked Dhoon, he didn't say anything to Dhoon Ramlogan directly.

He told his daughter to inform Dhoon he must provide other housing arrangements for her and their children.

Rajdaye appealed to Dhoon to help her find suitable housing for herself and all six children.

Dhoon Ramlogan, being found out, was the talk of the town and he was in a difficult situation. Dhoon's first child, a 19-year-old daughter with his legal wife, Jaya, was already married when I was born. His other children with Jaya still lived at the Ramlogan home.

He met with his parents, "Baap" and Moya (the Ramlogan matriarch) to confess to having a second family simultaneously while also having his arranged-marriage family with Jaya. Dhoon and the legal family lived on his parent's property as part of their extended household.

While they were upset, his parents Baap and Moya could not disown him outright because Dhoon was the eldest son in his family, a privileged position. Dhoon-Bai was already someone most people looked up to. Although he only completed fourth grade, he was a self-taught man and he could read and write. By reading newspapers, he kept up with current events, and let the community know what else was happening in the world. He was ambitious. He was a leader in the community.

Baap offered his son a building lot across the street from the main Ramlogan house, where Dhoon could put up a building to give Rajdaye and their newly-discovered grandchildren (Seeta and Mike) a place to live. However, Baap and Moya refused to allow Rajdaye's first four children to live there – especially, the two Muslim-fathered children.

Dhoon had to obey his parents. My mother's other children were not welcome because they were an embarrassment to them.

Eventually, my mother gave the two eldest children (Narine and Chandra) to her first husband and his relatives; and the third and fourth children (Sarah and Molly) to their father, Raj's lover Deen, to be raised by his family. At that time, she could not do any better. She did what she must to ensure everyone's survival.

PART II   THE VILLAGE OF CORIAL

Chapter 8: "Number 10" Demolished to Make a New House

Dhoon was in a difficult situation as well. He fathered two children in 1962; my brother Mike with his mistress Rajdaye; and my half-sister Sugars with his legal wife Jaya. When this became public knowledge, it caused gossip, resentment, and heartache to the women.

Mike and Sugars were born within a month of each other in July and August 1962. One infant in each house!

Finding no other alternate housing, Dhoon Ramlogan took Rajdaye, Mike and me to Corial, his hometown. Across the street from his parent on the sloping lot, he built a shell of a house for Rajdaye and their children (Mike and me).

Next to his parent's main house was the house where he lived with his current wife Jaya and their seven children still at home. Dhoon's older children justifiably resented their father having "his other woman and children" moved in across the street from their home. As a result, that side of the street and that side of the family hated my mother and us.

The home father built for us was small, but bigger than

Number 10. This new structure was on land Rajdaye was not in line to inherit. It would never be *her* property the way the real estate in Gasparillo at Number 10 would have been. However difficult her situation, Rajdaye was better off with Dhoon Ramlogan because of his decision to support and raise his children with her.

Here in Corial, father shared himself between two women in the two houses almost facing each other. Each night, it was his decision which house he would sleep in. No one seemed to know ahead of time in which one he would bed down, which woman he'd choose. He was living with his legal wife and children; and he was living with us, "his mistress and outside children."

His extended family didn't want to see Mike and me. We were an embarrassment. Seeing us flaunted dad and mom's disregard of the rules of society. His parents who were my paternal Grandfather Baap and Grandmother Moya especially didn't care for my brother and me. I don't remember any hugs or kisses from either of them like I got from Nanny Kasey and Grandpa Balkissoon.

Although living in their big house just across from ours, they didn't want anything to do with us. They made a point of showing their disapproval by not inviting us over, never even allowing us in their house, while they always welcomed father's first family.

My father's relatives yelled, "Go away!" whenever we crossed the street or got near their lawn.

ᘐ᠂ᘙ᠂ᘐ

Rajdaye's new house was constructed from lumber and materials from the house at Number 10 in Gasparillo, which was demolished. With our pregnant mother, my brother and I were moved into a palm-leaf thatched-roof house. It was bigger than Number 10. This new house was about 20-feet x 14-feet and had two rooms. Both were used as sleeping rooms. Cooking was done outside in an attached lean-to where the dishes and cooking utensils were stored, too.

The house was built with the front of the building supported by large bamboo poles. The shell of the house had wood-plank walls, chinked with a wattle-and-daub made of dirt, manure, and hay. Under the front of the house was a lanai, half the depth of the house. A lanai is a built-in open-front porch. Mother prepared the lanai's floor with a mud-and-cow-manure coating to seal the hard-packed dirt.

The lanai functioned as a sitting room, a shady place for the children to play, and adults to lounge in hammocks or on settees. She put up a clothesline there so clothes could dry away from the almost-daily afternoon rain.

She also made a U-shaped fire ring in the backyard by shaping dirt and cow manure on a stand called a *chula*. Three mounds of mud bricks in a U-shape held up the cooking pots. The fuel and fire went in the middle, and pots balanced on the earthen mounds.

We children helped to collect dry branches, twigs, and wood for the cooking fire.

ꜩ🐦ꜩ

In the morning, mother took my brother and me to a spring to collect fresh water and haul it back to fill our rain barrels. We didn't have running water or electricity at the time.

During the night when mother was sleeping, my half-sisters from the other side often came from across the street and kicked over our water barrels to show how unhappy they were with this public situation – having to put up with their father's "other woman" and illegitimate kids living across the street from the legitimate family.

The scorn, pranks, and animosity of Dhoon's other children increased. They didn't like Rajdaye, and eventually, she gave up trying to get them to like, accept, or even tolerate her.

ꜩ🐦ꜩ

Mom gave birth to my sister Geeta in 1964. We didn't have milk. The babies were breastfed and the youngest children were given the water drained from cooking rice, mixed with a bit of sugar. Raj used the Pepsi Cola· bottle with a rubber nipple over the top, or a smaller Coca-Cola· bottle. Of course, the rubber nipples were store-bought, and made to fit on the soda bottles.

36

ɞ⋅☙⋅ɞ

My brother and I were not permitted to go across the street to the grandparents, where the other family's children were given sweets, citrus, sugarcane, hugs, kisses, and lots of affection. We yearned for that attention.

Soon, someone from the other family would yell, "Go away! Don't look at us." Mike and I didn't understand. There was no place else for us to go.

Every workday my brother and I were put under the lemon tree to wait for mother to return from her job. She knew how to sew, wash and iron, and how to cut sugarcane. Mother was resourceful.

Sometimes when Mike and I were parked under the lemon tree, we noticed dad sneaking out, not wanting Jaya or his other children to see him leave our house.

Affectionately, our father patted Mike on the head and pulled on my pigtails, tugged on our noses, and winked. Then he'd hot-foot it back into Jaya's house before anyone else saw him. In those few moments we felt loved and included. We felt happy, as if we belonged.

My father took a big chance to move us to Corial. Only after I grew up, could I understand my grandparents Baap and Moya Ramlogan's, and their grandchildren's, harsh feelings toward my mother (but not toward our father).

After the move we were relocated across the street from their house. Our situation became a public embarrassment. I wished it could have been a smoother transition.

Chapter 9: The Ghost, 1968

In Corial, there were two characters called "Pepper Jack" and "Moon" who were notoriously heavy drinkers. In the small hours one morning coming home from binges, each took a short cut through the cemetery where each man collapsed in a drunken stupor – but neither one knew the other was there!

Moon awoke and discovered he had rested his head on a tombstone. Alarmed, he let out a yell, jumped up, and stumbled around to see whether he was dead or alive.

Hearing the strange noise, Pepper Jack opened his bleary eyes, got up fast and ran out of the cemetery.

When Moon heard something stirring and running, he looked up and saw a blur. He thought he saw a ghost flying away fast.

Moon jumped up and ran back to the village. Always talkative, from then on he told everybody: "There's a ghost living in the cemetery!"

୫ 👻 ୫

For years, we children were disciplined by that ghost story. Villagers and family told us a ghost would come snatch us if we didn't behave. Knowing others had seen the ghost there, we believed the warning.

When Mike and I sat under the lemon tree, we didn't

move an inch, afraid the ghost would come take us away!

The children in the village were afraid of the ghost, especially when they had to take the shortcut across the cemetery. After they'd crossed the cemetery and reached the village, they stayed put.

To cross that line again when the ghost already knew you were out and about, the ghost would surely come snatch you.

Chapter 10: Bringing them Home, c. 1969 & 1970

The house in Corial was my mother's home. She made it hers. She surfaced the floors and walls with a mixture of cow manure and mud. It hardened as it dried out. She planted flowers outside and put up two hammocks.

My dad built us a new outhouse.

She liked to organize the water buckets and barrels with downspouts to catch the maximum rain water for our use.

Rajdaye pressed Dhoon to bring home her other children (Molly, Sarah, and Narine) to Corial. He refused in order to keep peace with his parents.

Mother's oldest child Chandra moved to Corial to help mother care for us, but she also became one more mouth to feed. In addition, my father's parents did not want her in our house which situated on their land.

So my mother arranged for Chandra to work for a school teacher that she used to iron clothes for. My 10-year-old sister Chandra was employed for that family as a servant, a housekeeper, and babysitter. She worked there until she was 15 and her marriage was arranged.

She was paid $2.00/week which she gave to our mother who used it to buy milk for the babies. The money for milk and food was a great blessing. Chandra was always there for us.

Chapter 11: The First TV in the Village

Mr. Manny Chand's success was visible. He owned a big house with electricity, a couple of big trucks, and was known as the richest man in Corial. In the late 1960s, he was the first person in the village to own a television. The black-and-white TV screen was small, maybe a 13-inch screen.

The government owned the telecommunications service and broadcasted programs over its public TV station several hours a day.

Mr. Manny shared his good fortune. He rigged the TV with extension cords and brought it outside after work.

More than 50 people of Corial crowded on the Manny family's lawn to view programs on that tiny screen. Children sat in the front and the adults sat behind them. There, we saw "Little House on the Prairie," "Macmillan and Wife," and on Saturdays, an hour-long Indian program of song and dance, called "Mastanabahar."

It changed the pace of living. People did their housework and chores with renewed energy during the day to be free to walk up the street to watch one television show. The TV shows lasted 30 or 60 minutes a day. We never stayed longer than an hour. By the end of the program, it was usually dark. We went home feeling great to be connected to the rest of the world and to have viewed the latest wonder of the world–television!

❦

Watching Western TV shows gave me the idea that there was something outside of my village and one day I would get to see the bigger world.

I learned from Mr. Manny that when he was doing well in life, he shared his success with the rest of the village.

Life was not as hard when people shared.

Chapter 12: Our Early Elementary School Education

Mike and I were fortunate the British built an elementary school for us. From the age 5 to 11 years of age, we attended this Presbyterian school.

We did not have shoes or socks to wear. It did not matter to us. We were happy to walk bare footed and be able to play in the rain puddles on our way to and from school.

Mike and Seeta revisit Brothers Presbyterian School in 2008. The school is in the background. In the foreground is an area for students to wait for rides.

ཏ☙ཏ

My dad decided one day to make us shoes. He and our
mother took old tires and cut them to fit our feet, poked holes
in them with an ice pick and cut strips of leather to make shoe
laces which he attached to the shoes with a gigantic needle.
Mother had all of us helping to pull the needles through the
rubber. She even put the needles in her teeth to pull it by
backing up. We though it was a fun time making the shoes,
but unfortunately, they didn't hold up long.

Chapter 13: The Economy of the Village

In village life, sharing, caring, bartering, doing things as a group was a form of mutual aid and survival.

Through kinship ties, one could barter for almost any service. Each person strove to have a unique in-demand skill that would benefit the extended family and the community. To survive in such an economy, one must be innovative and creative. In Corial, we had more cousins. Father's relatives lived throughout the village and each person had a skill. One was a barber; another was a carpenter.

Villagers didn't have much cash. People reserved their T&T dollar to buy things like dry goods such as fabric, hardware, staples, and necessities such as rice and flour.

Clothes were usually hand-me-downs. Laundry was hung to dry on a clothesline or spread on the shrubbery.

Mother insisted we go to bed early enough so the kerosene lamps didn't need to be turned on.

There was sharing of any abundance. During harvest, people hand-picked crops. Pickers brought whole peas by the bucket back to the village, where they and others shelled the peas as a group. The entire group shared the shelled peas equally.

People also grew other food crops and raised livestock. By sharing the earth's bounty, people survived. In our village, it was not unusual to use garden produce such as fresh peas in place of cash. A person could get a haircut for a certain quantity of fresh peas. A haircut or a quantity of fresh peas could be swapped for something else depending on abundance at the time or how your talent was valued by the village. Someone else could make a little bench. That's how the village economy thrived.

Coconut is a staple of our economy. The coconut milk and water are prized as a refreshing beverages. The pulp of young coconuts is called "jelly" and is delicious and nutritious. The solidified jelly was used to make sweets. Coconut oil was used as a moisturizer for skin and a hair conditioner. My mom taught us if we were poor and down on our luck, "The coconut will feed you. It is your friend." The leaves from the coconut trees were used to make brooms which could be bartered for other goods. Sitting in the shade of the trees, we made brooms and, from the coconut husks, fashioned baskets, bowls, and cups. It was a relaxing social gathering for everyone. It was also a time of courtship and suitors for the teenagers to have a date "to make brooms" under the watchful eyes of parents.

Ladies in the village often sat together for a day and pulled the fiber out of dry coconut husks and used the softer fibers to make mattresses. The heart fiber was used to scrub dishes. The stuffed mattress bags were spread along the road to cure. Sometimes smaller bags like pillow cases were stuffed with rice. The children had to walk on them to loosen the husks from the rice.

The elders knew how to use their talents for creative things. They used simple materials, such as tiny corn husks, to teach us how to make dolls. For Christmas, small children received corn-husk dolls made with husk pieces sticking out as arms and legs. Such a doll was often our only toy.

There is a fruit called the tamarind. It has a little seed. After eating the fruit, the seeds were saved and later sewn into a scrap of cloth to make bean bags for us to play with. I fondly remember playing with beanbags and corn dollies.

Chapter 14: Jaya's Death in 1971

In 1971, there was a tragedy we kids didn't understand. Our father's legal wife Jaya died, leaving seven children. This was our first close experience with a person's death. Father's children were crushed, and my mother was blamed for Jaya's death.

Although Jaya's teenage children didn't like his mistress, Dhoon knew Rajdaye was loyal to him and would help him with their care as best she could.

Father didn't have the luxury of sinking into a complicated bereavement because he had to care for his unmarried children by his now-dead wife, as well as four children of his mistress. He had his hands full. There was no handbook for him to follow to point out the pitfalls of blending families. Without discussing it with Rajdaye, after Jaya's death, father decided to *blend* his two families together. While it may have seemed like a sensible idea to him, believing it would be "easier" to have all of his children together, this was real trouble!

At least, he took it in small steps. After work in the evenings, Rajdaye's children were required to go with him to where his other children were spending the evening on hammocks and benches.

They acted as if we were intruders, and our mother would never step foot on what she viewed as Jaya's property. She felt out of place.

At this point, he began to beat Rajdaye frequently and neighbors noticed, but no one in his family came to her defense. Rajdaye's sisters and brothers who were old enough to take a taxi came to Corial to speak to him about why he should not use violence to vent his frustrations. The family understood that he was left with his seven motherless children. They offered to take Rajdaye and all her children back to Gasparillo if that would ease his burden.

Raydaye refused because she loved Dhoon and wanted to be with him.

Our father realized more than ever that he was caught in the middle. He was pressured by the older kids of his first family who made it clear they wanted him to leave my mother and her children (us). But he stuck by us.

Eventually, he merged all of us together in his house — but only for about six months. The bedlam that started in those six months continued for the next 11 years.

To placate his first seven children, Mr. Dhoon realized he could not marry my mother, because in Jaya's children's eyes that would have been the ultimate betrayal of their now-deceased mother. Only one child was married when Jaya died. Those who remained at home did not approve of my mother. His kids blamed him, often saying, "Our mother died of a broken heart and you and that woman caused it!"

With their mother gone, it was an especially sad time for them. They had not really had time to grieve. It was also difficult for our father.

Mother, in return, pressured my father to be less involved with his nearly-grown kids. That upset him.

It was painful, because we knew at that point that we were in the middle, too; we were considered to be *the problem.* Had it not been for us, maybe mother could have gone back to her family.

During this transition, I watched my dad and learned from his mistakes. At a young age, I realized my father was an imperfect man, but we loved and cherished him. He had a way about him. He realized that he did wrong by the circumstances that led to having so many children and two spouses living side by side, but he also tried to make it right. He was torn between the two families he had made. However, he developed a unique relationship with each of his kids and loved us all. He tried to be fair.

At the time, nobody cared for anybody. The arguments and dividing line had been drawn. Mother didn't especially like Jaya's children because some were teenagers in the rebellious stage. They resented us and didn't want younger kids around. The teens often ordered us out and made sure we felt unwanted.

It was stressful; all day long, there was fighting and squabbling between him and my mother, as well as among those older kids and my siblings. How could father expect these two sets of people to live in the same house? Even his own family, his brothers and sisters told him it was not a good idea.

Next, he decided to take some of his older teenagers, and

try to place them with some of his deceased wife's family. This didn't work either!

Nobody wanted to have so many kids, especially not resentful teenagers.

I knew my mother and father were struggling to make ends meet and they had a lot of hardships in meeting the challenges of day to day life.

Chapter 15: Rajdaye's Fateful Decision

At the time of Jaya's death, Jaya had seven living children and our mother had eight children of her own.

Mother found a new maturity and resignation. She realized this was it for her. She didn't have the energy or time to date anyone else or try to find some other man to marry her.

Rajdaye was back in the situation she had been earlier. A woman with four small children of her own, and eight all together. She made a conscious decision to stay with dad for better or for worse.

She recognized she would have been better off if she'd had an education. She had never been given the opportunity to learn to read or write. She vowed to make education possible for her children.

At the time, in Trinidad and Tobago, that was a huge promise because an education was not a universal right, and higher education was a privilege given only to the superior scholars from "the best families."

Chapter 16: Arranged Marriages

Arranged Marriages were part of the culture and traditions that Indians continued after they immigrated to Trinidad and Tobago. Sometimes arranged marriages work, sometimes they don't. With arranged marriages, your parents looked for someone compatible from the same socioeconomic background as yours. My parents wanted the arranged marriages for each of us to be within our own culture and religion.

Parents know when you're ready. Most parents would notice if one daughter was a little more sexy, a little more adventurous, a little more liable to experiment, or more attracted to boys. As a parent, you know your child. It wasn't just that the couple had to be right – it's not an age, it's a stage. It's a phase. A certain level of maturity and awakening about the opposite sex.

Arranged marriages usually lasted when parents understood that particular child and chose wisely. The parents are aware when a child is interested in having a relationship. The assumption is if the parents can make it possible for these children to remain married to their first love, the partner of their first physical intimacy, it creates a bond of emotional intimacy that lasts – especially when the union is reinforced by a social culture and family ties. The families and the culture help the partners economically and socially to remain married.

People misunderstand the concept of arranged marriage. It's not the arbitrary plucking of someone off the street. The parent(s) look at the qualities of the person, the personality and temperament, and ability to provide. The parents want to make sure there's a match even when opposites attract. They look for someone who will complement their child. Good qualities such as strength, emotional stability, good assets, and resources – maybe land, a good family, and other evidence of being able to provide for a family. Beauty was generally defined as girls with lighter-skin and long thick hair.

My father loved all his children and was close to them. He wanted all his children, especially his daughters, to marry well. He took his responsibility for this seriously.

He didn't take the responsibility after Jaya's death to make Rajdaye his legal wife, not just his common law wife.

In the 1960s and '70s, parents concentrated their resources on their boys and this, too, helped them to make a good match. Typically, to enter into an arranged marriage, a young man had to prove himself to be a good prospect, needed a piece of land, a good job, a good name, integrity, and the potential to build a home – having a home meant you could start a family.

Mother always said, "Don't have sex outside of marriage. Make sure you're married." She never explained what "having sex" was. It was just why they wanted all the daughters to be married ahead of time.

All mother said to us was, "Until you are married, don't go near a boy."

We had no knowledge of "sex education." No one ever spoke of "birth control." All we knew was what we had been told that, "If you go near a boy, something bad is going to happen." We were also told in the same tone of voice, "Don't wear a bathing suit. Don't let people see your skin. Don't let anyone see your legs, your breasts, or your arms – only your feet, or your face. Be modest."

In my family, it was considered wiser to spend the money on the boys and their education and vocational training. Girls must be taught to cook, clean, and do laundry and child care. Being married into a good family was the ultimate goal set for daughters. Girls were viewed as more of an expense who would eventually go live with her husband's family.

My father was very selective about suitable marriage partners for their children. One by one the older siblings were married off, and each time he had one less mouth to feed, clothe, and shelter.

Chapter 17: Chandra's Wedding

Around 1972, we had both families living with us or in close proximity. Dad became preoccupied with arranging marriages for his teenaged daughters. Finding suitable prospects became a challenge.

Weddings and attendance at Hindu temple were social highlights for our family. I watched the procedural arrangements with curiosity and pride. I learned there Hindu prayers and religious songs known as *bhajans*.

My mother's daughter Chandra was the first marriage that my father arranged for his step-children. He chose Dhanpaul from Ben Lomond. He and Chandra lived in Ben Lomond after their marriage.

Dan is a wise man we all look up to, an adviser, and a pillar in our family. Even now, Chandra and Dan remain married and have four children.

Little did we know, Dan would change the fortune of all of us. Dan told Dhoon about a piece of property fronting on the main street in Ben Lomond that was for sale. It included a variety store with a two-story residence behind it.

Part III Ramlogan's Dry Goods Store in Ben Lomond

Sometime in 1973, through Chandra's new family, Dhoon negotiated for the purchase of the variety shop and residence from Mister Jim. My father moved *everybody* out of the house at Corial into that shop in Ben Lomond. Leaving the village of his ancestors caused a big transition. With our blended family living in the shop building, it was crowded.

When father purchased the store, he soon found he could no longer also be a full-time police officer (estate police) on call 24/7 as he had been in Corial. Managing the store in Ben Lomond was a full time occupation. When he resigned from his job as a policeman, he proudly announced to the family, "Now, I am a businessman!" However, it also meant he was giving up having a regular dependable paycheck.

Mother loved the ritual of getting his uniform ready and laying it out on the bed for him each morning. He was proud of the way she ironed it and in this way helped to make him look more handsome and important. My mother wept when he hung up the uniform for good.

After the British left, local people had to take over, to set up a new system of local government – similar to a City Council in the U.S.A. In Corial and Ben Lomond, Dhoon served as a village elder. The village held *Panchait,* a village meeting conducted periodically by the village elders to discuss public matters such as water rights, public works, and public safety.

Wherever Dhoon Ramlogan lived, he would be included as a voting member of the *Panchait.* My dad took an active role in the village, especially concerning infrastructure planning and capital improvements.

My parents were an inspiration to many. My ambition stemmed from their example.

࿐❦࿐

The move to Ben Lomond and the property was a God-send. It became a springboard for each of us into a better future. After our move to Ben Lomond, dad soon received offers of marriage for his other daughters.

࿐❦࿐

Ben Lomond was a busy place. While there were fewer pedestrians, there was heavy vehicular traffic and private taxicabs. The road itself was wider and paved. Sugar cane workers crowded the roads with cars and trucks. Even carts pulled by donkeys and bulls hauled the cane.

From a child's viewpoint, I needed to learn the faces and names of all the new neighbors and customers.

The town became the place where the blended-Ramlogan family advanced socially and financially. There people respected my dad, and they came to respect all his children. My father became an elder in the village.

Chapter 18: Eggplants and Bananas

Invitations for weddings were not usually mailed because customarily parents walked door to door to invite each guest personally. Sometimes donations of cash or garden vegetables would be received to help offset the expenses.

A tent would be set up with bamboo poles and tarpaulins to make a place for the ceremony and party. The bride and groom normally dressed up in rented or borrowed wedding attire. Generally, a wedding was performed at the bride's home and the village helped with the extraordinary amount of vegetarian food that was prepared for the reception.

On the eve of my step-sister Toya's wedding, when I was around ten, my girlfriends and I secretly snuck into the farewell party for the bride the night before the wedding. There we observed the invited women of the village singing and dancing, while making gestures about sexual acts with bananas and other fruit intended wordlessly to teach the bride sex education. Eggplants and bananas ruled, but always covered with squares of cloth representing the bed sheets. A bride was never told anything else. The mature wives were giggling throughout the sexual enactment.

Chapter 19: Places for Everything & Everyone: Toothbrushes, c. 1970

In Ben Lomond, we woke up smiling and reflected that in Corial, we didn't have toothbrushes. There before school, mother broke a branch from a non-poisonous bush, and bit twigs to fray the fibers into brushes. She knew twigs, such as the ones from the black-sage bush, would fray the right way and were safe.

When Mister Jim owned the small shop, he sold groceries and some toiletries. The stock was sold with the transaction. The toiletries included an assortment of new toothbrushes! We thought of them as our "Welcome to Ben Lomond" gift!

Several days after we'd moved in, my father called all the children together for a meeting, which he called, "A discussion of socioeconomics."

He gathered all the toothbrush stock and presented each of us with a personal toothbrush and instructed us to brush our teeth with salt. The gift of a toothbrush didn't include toothpaste. We were to label our personal toothbrush.

After the toothbrushes were distributed, dad herded us outside. He drove nails through a board, and used pliers to bend these exposed nails into hooks. Then, using other nails, he nailed the board of hooks to the side of the house. He lined us up by age, then assigned each person a personal hook on which to hang their prized toothbrush. The eldest one got the first hook, and so forth. Although I was the ninth child of my father, I had the fifth or sixth hook because some siblings had married and no longer lived at home.

When we received our first toothbrushes, we felt like brushing our teeth all day! Those toothbrushes were as precious as diamonds! My toothbrush and its hook were among the few things I could call mine.

I learned the value of caring for personal property. I learned so much from my father through simple things like that.

From our family, we learned an important lesson: that although poverty is an inconvenience, poverty does not necessarily breed crime. It generates love.

Was our glass half-full, or half-empty?

I look at privileged kids in the U.S.A. and in Trinidad who have everything, and I feel much is lacking from their lives that we had *because of our poverty*. Our poverty forged a common bond, because we had instinctively a common purpose, the basic instinct to survive and fend for the younger siblings.

If you know how to convert all the negatives into self-motivation, it is the greatest inspiration to success.

 za ❦ za

A typical day in Ben Lomond included our little army doing chores quickly in an orderly fashion. I peeled vegetables and swept the courtyard, my sisters made beds, and mother and my sisters Toya, Sugars, Curtis, and Geeta cooked. Geeta and Ling took care of trash and Mike helped my father get the car ready.

After chores, we changed into our school uniforms we'd ironed and pressed the night before. There usually weren't enough socks to go around, so we took turns wearing the socks; most had holes in them. At first, I did not have any. It wasn't exactly an equitable distribution. Most of the time, the shoes and socks were really for Ling and Geeta, because they were younger and the socks were small. I didn't have shoes and socks then.

Cash money was scarce for our parents, but barter was still good currency. Father bartered rides for us with taxi drivers by giving old T-shirts in lieu of payment. Mother gave good towels to barter several months of rides to and from school.

za ❦ za

Several times a week my father went to San Fernando to buy goods on credit. He brought the goods back in the car– flour, and rice, whatever. When he got to the garage, the children had to off-load. But we did it with such pride! We

wanted to see what he'd purchased. Batteries, hair ties –
whatever he brought home – would go into the shop. Mother
also helped him to unpack and stock the shelves in the shop.

She cleaned the shop, swept it, and shined the
countertops. Dad kept the records and attended to the
customers. He was smart and made a good living.

One of us would go into the shop and direct where
everything was going to go. He was pretty organized with the
shop. The boys would carry the big, heavy flour sacks, and
the girls would carry the lighter items.

He had good credit with his wholesalers, but he often
spoke of "the bank overdraft" from the previous week which
needed to be covered.

Even so, dad allowed customers to buy goods on credit
and a promise to pay off the total whenever the customer got
paid. This was good business sense. When the customer came
back to make a payment, he'd usually buy more.

For example, father sold alcohol by the drink, and he
opened a pack of cigarettes to sell the cigarettes individually.
He made more profit that way.

Dad also believed that no one should go hungry. He gave
away a lot, but he made it back with sales.

We sold daily newspapers in the store. The change in his
attitude and in how people treated him came about partly
because he had access to more than one newspaper, such as
the *Trinidad Express* and *The Guardian*. Before school, he
gathered all the children into the shop, and closed the door.
That way, mother could not come in, or call us back to do

more chores. He let each of us select a newspaper to read.

He took this opportunity to ask us questions and we would debate what we read. In this way, he was teaching us world politics. We children developed a love for reading, politics, and world news because of dad.

ઠ❧ઠ

Deciding what to make to feed so many was a challenge. Most of the time, we had fresh pita bread and a vegetable. Mother would wake me up before the others calling, "Seeta! Garlic, onions, potatoes. Let's go peel 'em."

Only after the peeling was completed, would she awaken Geeta, Ling, and Sugars. Before school, their jobs were to sweep the courtyard, pack lunches, and help make bread.

In addition to getting this work done, there was always a line to use the bathroom.

There weren't enough cups, plates, or spoons to go around. We re-used the empty beverage cans to drink from, and ate with our hands in the traditional Indian manner.

We were quite creative. I sometimes wonder how we survived.

Every minute had to be planned, and someone had to take charge, which mother usually did. She was exasperated, and yelled at us frequently.

On Sundays in Ben Lomond, father went to the open air markets to haggle with vendors for the least expensive price for vegetables, such as eggplant, tomatoes, peppers, corn and

65

potatoes.

Although we were Hindu, my father did permit us to eat chicken. He purchased one chicken a week from a vendor's stall, where we pointed out the chicken we wanted. The vendor would catch and weigh it to determine the price.

At home, we had to butcher and prepare it. My sister Geeta was the queen of butchering any fowl or livestock. For a chicken, she first cut the neck, chopped off the head and legs, drained the blood, gutted it, plucked it, and removed the pin feathers, all so it could be cooked. Mother saw to it that the fleshy parts, like the leg, thigh, and breasts, were cut into very small pieces so we could each have a taste of meat. She cooked the pieces in a stew or a pot of curry. Our Sunday meal was typically red beans, rice and stewed chicken.

We had a dining table but it was reserved for dad and the elder siblings. Mother served dad his dinner first, then the older kids before the younger ones. The rest of us got a plate of food and sat on the steps, windowsills, or on the bare floor leaning against a wall. We listened to "The American Top-40-Hits" and "The Hit Parade" from our one and only radio.

If we were good that week, we were each served a piece of chicken with meat on it; if we were bad, we got a bone. Mother waited until father had eaten. After he was satisfied and everyone else had been served, only then did she eat, always standing up.

We rarely had extra food for second helpings. Most of the time, we ate whatever was prepared, or we did not eat. Many meal times were ruined by the bickering over who had received a larger share, and why that one deserved it. I almost always got the backbone or a chicken foot because I dared to question everything and anything.

I remember bartering with my sisters to get a good piece, a bigger piece with chicken meat. I bargained that if I got a wing, or a piece of the breast, I'd help that sibling with the laundry. It worked sometimes when one felt sorry for me.

I recall telling my mother, "One day, when I grow up, I will buy and eat an entire chicken just for myself."

She said, "I hope you do."

But I never have.

In our family and other families like us, beverage cups were scarce. In order to have as many as we needed, my father took the condensed milk cans and fold the edges down with a hammer. That way, each child could have a cup.

My mother wanted a cheese grater but we could not afford to buy one, so father took the tops of aluminum cans and poked holes in them to make cheese graters for us.

We didn't have an oven, so he cut a 55-gallon drum in half and hinged the halves together to make a rotisserie oven in our backyard. He put a galvanized platform on the top were we could bake Christmas cakes and other treats.

Mother used all available space in the yard to grow vegetables such as tomatoes, eggplant, hot peppers, okra, and corn. It was watered with water from our rain-water cistern.

ꙮ

We accepted our fate, being from a huge family, and trying our best to make it work. We did complain among each other, but also encouraged each other.

Mother was very strict. With so many children under one roof, parents had to be strict. I think we all learned to cope and be organized because mom stressed doing things the right way the first time.

ꙮ

When it rained, we had a different household schedule. Each child stood in a designated spot and held a bucket under a certain leak in the roof. Mine was a huge leak and therefore my bucket filled up first. I had to empty the bucket of rainwater outside in the rain where I used the opportunity to take a shower. At first, this made the other bucket-holders jealous. Only when a bucket filled, was that child permitted to go outside to dump it. Some kids took water from another's bucket to make a full bucket so as to be free to play outside. We soon used it as a happy occasion to dance and sing in the rain. We made everything fun.

ꙮ

Electricity was rationed and we needed to know what time it would be on and what to do whenever the electricity was shut off. We had to round up our brothers and sisters before it got dark, but if it was in the evening, my sisters would call out, "Seeta, flash you teeth so we can find you."

In the beginning, only a few households had electricity or electric or gas-fueled clothes dryers. After our clothes dried outside, each of us had a cardboard box in which to put our folded garments. Mother spot checked the boxes each evening to be sure we had them neat and tidy and if we the box of clothes was messy, she would punish us by using a belt on our bottoms. I always got the most licks because I was the most disobedient.

We made our own lanterns with kerosene in pop bottles, old clothing for wicks. They were very dangerous, so most of the time when it was dark outside, mother put us to bed in the dark.

Laundry was hung outside on clotheslines or spread on the shrubbery to dry. Many years later, we got electricity in the shop, and then in the house.

At night, mother made us a thin porridge of Quaker Oats to drink. She tended to her garden so we could have the food; all this in addition to minding the shop and doing the cleaning. Her work never ended.

Later we owned a few kerosene lamps, but they were never to be used because we had electricity by then. Mother insisted we were all tucked into bed at dusk so that lighting a lamp would be unnecessary. She believed "spending the kerosene" was an expense only the wasteful wealthy dared to fritter away.

We slept three or four of us at a time in the beds. Our mattresses were a duvet fabric stuffed with coconut fiber. Mother harvested and dried coconuts, then tore the husks apart to pull coconut fiber to stuff into the duvets to make mattresses.

The mattress I shared with three siblings had a huge tear in the fabric where the stuffing had thinned. We'd plug the hole in the mattress with our house clothes to keep the fiber in the mattress, and then wore those crumpled clothes to play the next day. We didn't dare use school uniforms this way.

In Ben Lomond, mother made friends with other women who belonged to the same Hindu temple, and they often went to temple as a group. It was one of the few opportunities mother had to see people outside the shop or the home.

When she had a free minute, mother took the same interest in the seven of us that she had with my dad. Perhaps more so me; she put a lot of pressure on me because I was the eldest of her girls living with her and my dad. She had fun with us and wanted to accompany us wherever we went.

Unfortunately, my mother did not put the energy into spending quality time with my father's younger children, and this became a subject of contention.

Chapter 20: The Neighbor's Outhouse

I was ten years of age when I met Mrs. Marahjin, a dignified, elderly, Indian widow who lived next door to us. She lived by herself and was very religious. In her own right, she held the title of "Maharajan," a rank designation of people very high in our caste system.

Villagers remarked, "Her husband died and left her here."

She dressed stylishly with the scarf around her head and a long dress. She was also a very light-skinned woman – a nice-looking lady.

I decided to attempt to make friends with her, but mother cautioned me, "Be careful. We are new here, and we don't know her very well."

With that, I was all the more determined to get to know her. I looked for ways to bring her food.

The difference between our Corial outhouse and the Ben Lomond outhouse was the manner of construction. In Corial, what we had was made out of mismatched boards and a piece of galvanized metal tacked up this way and that. Mother just hung up a piece of cloth for privacy, hoping nobody else would see.

In those days during the night, it was customary for people

to use a chamberpot. Nobody had indoor toilets then. Even in Corial, we had a chamberpot for use overnight.

But in Ben Lomond, we had an outhouse with a door. It was a step up. By now, we had at least 12 kids in our house, plus mother and father, all sharing a one-seater outhouse.

After I visited Mrs. Marahjin a few times, she asked me to empty the chamberpot for her. "If you agree to do this favor for me, you may come and sit with me," Mrs. Marahjin said, as if she were telling me a big secret.

"Yes, Mrs. Marahjin, I can do that." I nodded my head.

She didn't tell me where to dump it, and I feared it would be impudent to ask. While our place had an outhouse where I could dump it, it was always in use by my brothers and sisters. Worse, many times our outhouse had big frogs or snakes in it! At least, we periodically cleaned the outhouse with a disinfectant called Detol.

We had a system in place. If one of us had to use the outhouse at night, it was a group effort. One would hold the flashlight or flambeau, one would carry the salt, and another would assist any younger child who had to go. The salt was applied to the backs of the frogs who were waiting for us in there.

There seemed like no special place outside to empty Mrs. Marahjin's chamberpot. I discovered an empty lot beside her house where I could dump it in the weeds. When I told her where I had dumped it, she explained where her outhouse was. I was amazed. As a widow living alone, she had not only her own private outhouse, but also a full bathroom that went with it!

If I become friends with her, from time to time maybe I could use her outhouse. I'll have a good place to go without competing with so many other people.

It was worth it to me to trade emptying her chamber pot for my use of her private outhouse.

Her place wasn't like ours. It was always nice and dry.

The next time I visited her, we had the first of many conversations about her fascinating but difficult life. Her world was much bigger than mine! It gave me a desire to travel. Time with Mrs. Marahjin became something I looked forward to. She told me stories about India, and the families who journeyed from Bihar, India to Trinidad and Tobago.

When it was time to leave, she again asked me to dump her chamberpot. All the while, I loved the individual attention. *Little did I know, my association with Mrs. Marahjin would influence the rest of my life.*

Chapter 21: Monkey's Dignity

An Indian man in the village had the facial features resembling a monkey, so the local people called him, "Monkey." Children coming home from school teased him, threw rocks at him, and taunted him.

Although he was born into an established middle-class family, because of his facial features, his family did not seem to give him the support he needed.

One day, Monkey came into our store foul-smelling. My father took him into the backyard where we had a shower and a bathroom. He gave Monkey a bath, a shave, a trim, and clean clothes. He taught him about using the plumbing facilities in the bathroom.

After that, Monkey walked miles each day to come to our house, and my father would go through that entire routine. My dad did that every day for years until old Monkey got sick and he died.

Although we sold the newspapers in our store, each morning Monkey would bring a newspaper under his arm for my father.

My father didn't have the heart to tell him he didn't need the newspaper. He took it, and showed appreciation. He read that newspaper, even if he'd read the day's paper earlier in the morning.

The entire village respected Monkey after that, and

respected my dad. Because here was a man who took the time to take care of another human being, and in so doing he instilled a lot of love and charity in many other people in our village.

These are the little things my dad did that made us wonder about the complex behavior of human beings.

He had his own way about him that was totally endearing. We all learned to be leaders from him.

Chapter 22: Curtis, the Shampoo Queen

There was no predictable, steady, cash flow for our household, only what came into the store from sales and was left after expenses were paid.

Father had a strict rule: *Anything I buy to stock the shop is my inventory. You kids are not supposed to take any of MY INVENTORY!*

The rule made us resourceful. If we wanted to "take" sweets from the shop, we formed a food chain, where one child was designated to take the sweets and pass it to another. Then we shared the loot upstairs.

Mother supplied us with sodas when father was not looking. When father let us have sodapop, he diluted it with milk first.

If he caught one of his daughters with nail polish or shampoo, she would be in big trouble. Imagine an extended household of 12 females and at least 11 males, not including aunts and uncles. Now imagine all our thick, black, Indian hair and no shampoo, only laundry soap.

Of course, there were things girls really needed, so we stole from the store when necessary.

Dad didn't want us to take shampoo because he had to pay

a lot for it, and he feared we'd deplete his stock. The shampoo sold in his store did not come in bottles but in tiny single-use packets printed with the brand name, "Helene Curtis."

Rakhi always had the most wavy, shiny, beautiful hair. Dad knew she had to be pilfering shampoo, but looked the other way as a small way of showing his love. Dad nicknamed my half-sister Rakhi "Curtis" from the brand of shampoo. Others claimed it was because she had a crush on a boy named Curtis.

Curtis and I became the ringleaders getting the shampoo for the others. We tip-toed into the shop, and snatched one shampoo packet each day to share among all of us girls – five of us shampooed our hair by sharing one tablespoonful of shampoo from a packet.

Curtis would sneak in the store to get a tube of toothpaste and rationed it among us. A tube of toothpaste was harder to hide than a small packet of shampoo. If I was getting along with her that week, she would let me use her tube of toothpaste. Other times she hid that precious tube under her pillow, where she thought we couldn't get it.

Dad's store sold small metal hair clips we used to pin our hair back. He wasn't as strict with them because we could use them and put them back into the display case. My job was to put them back without any stray hairs attached.

To survive, we had to be clever to obtain necessities or to find what we needed in that shop.

Curtis looked out for Mike and me. She gave me a lot of hugs. For example, if mother lashed out at me for talking back, or for not doing my homework, when I couldn't find Mike, I'd go to Curtis.

She'd say, "Come. I'll protect you."

Once in a while, dad gave us a loaf of sliced bread (not regular flat bread), sardines, or other special food from the shop as a treat.

Chapter 23: Hair, Fashion, and Sanitary Napkins

After seeing Farrah Fawcett on TV, I wrote to the Hollywood Studios for a picture of Farrah and another from *Little House on the Prairie.* I waited three months for a reply.

By the time I was 15, I had long hair that reached down to my hips. Without permission, I cut it to a tapered shoulder length to look like Farrah Fawcett's hair style. Boy, did I get into trouble!

Mother cornered me that night. "You have no business cutting your hair. You will never find a husband with that short hair! It makes you look ugly. You defy our traditions!" In front of my sisters and brothers, she whipped me with a belt.

In our culture, a girl's long, thick hair was her beauty. For a girl to cut her hair was to defy society. I broke the rules when I cut my hair short – especially into an American style. Worse yet, I'd chopped it so badly, mother had to pay a hairdresser to fix the cut, and Mother cried about the expense.

For a daughter's birthday, mom might buy several yards of fabric and make her daughter a new dress. If we needed new outfits for a special occasions such as when invited to weddings or events in the village, dad bought material in bulk and mom sewed the same design for each of the girls – *I*

thought we looked like factory workers in uniform.

As time went by and we grew older, we preferred more fashionable styles of dress than she would pick out. Sometimes she could pay a seamstress to sew a nicer dress for a daughter's birthday.

Except for special occasions, we didn't wear saris. They were too expensive for everyday wear. We only wore them to the Hindu temple or for meeting a suitor's family.

The older people had a lot of rules and regulations for wearing traditional garb. A married woman had to cover her head. She couldn't show her skin – except when wearing a sari it was acceptable to show a bare midriff.

After I cut my hair, I changed my style of clothing. Without my parents approval, I became bolder in wearing shorter clothes and showing more skin but still remaining respectable.

I took scissors and cut away most of the fabric on the shoulders of my dress to make spaghetti straps. It caused a stir. I had seen this style on American TV programs such as *Charlie's Angels*, and I wanted to do things were popular in "the West."

ᨑ᭙ᨑ

For most people in Trinidad, cameras were not readily available. Formal family portraits were taken in a photographer's studio. Parents planned ahead to mark a special occasion. It was a rarity; we kids didn't know what it was all about. Only parents knew what special occasions were to be commemorated. Therefore, culturally taking a photograph was viewed as a luxury.

With eight sisters in the same house, our periods usually came close together. It was an ordeal to maintain cleanliness. While my father sold sanitary napkins in his store, he would not permit us to have any. Instead, mother ripped up old sheets into squares, similar to diapers, and gave each girl a bundle of 12 squares and showed us how to fold them into a pad. When soiled, we washed them with blue soap, rinsed them, and put the pieces of cloth on a chicken-wire drying stand father put up in the yard so they could dry in the sun. We had to make sure none of our brothers knew were having periods. At times, we used fig leaves to cover the cloth pads on the drying rack.

When our periods were finished, mother inspected our bundles of 12 to make sure the fabric was clean before storing them for the next month.

All the while, we yearned to take supplies of sanitary pads from our father's store.

Chapter 24: Christmas in Ben Lomond

We were blessed to be raised on an island where all religions were celebrated by everyone. We showed respect, tolerance, harmony, and promoted peace and goodwill.

As Hindu children, we celebrated *Diwali*, the festival of lights. We offered prayers to Mother Lakshmi to bless us and everyone on earth with health, wealth, and prosperity. Our father took pride in making us stands in which we would light our *deyas*, we sang religious songs, attended Hindu temple, and offered prayers. It was customary for non-Hindus to visit Hindu temples and homes to share in the festivities, vegetarian meals and sweets.

One of the joys of Diwali nights was strolling through the village watching the deyas being lit and hearing the Hindi music.

My mother also made sweets so we could celebrate the Muslim holiday of *Eid* to show appreciation for the Muslims in our family and country.

We children also noticed that most Christian people in Ben Lomond decorated their homes and put up Christmas trees. Although we were Hindu, we wanted to join in those festivities.

Our father was a practicing Hindu but believed in the Ten Commandments and the teachings of Jesus, so he didn't stop us.

We asked him for money to purchase a Christmas tree and decorations. That first year in Ben Lomond, we could not afford to buy them. However, father came up with a plan that if we would save all the foil wrappings from the cigarette boxes and gum wrappers, we could use the foil to make decorations for the tree the following Christmas. So all the children were on a mission to save foil year around. We hounded the customers to buy cigarettes and gum so we could get at the foil.

The following Christmas season, our father cut a dry branch and stuck it into a paint can secured upright with rocks.

We foiled the paint can, its "trunk" and the branches, and we had enough left to wrap empty match boxes and hung them on our tree. We were very proud of it.

In the spirit of Christmas, our father splurged and bought Christmas cookies, five apples, and a pound of grapes. He gave each of us a slice of apple and a little bunch of grapes, a tradition that we continued year after year regardless of our economic circumstances.

We danced to music on the radio to celebrate Carnival a time of festivities in Trinidad and Tobago. We made costumes for the occasion.

Chapter 25: Jumping to the Wrong Conclusions

I remember the day as if it were yesterday. One of my sisters developed a friendship with a boy our parents didn't approve of. When our parents discovered her friendship, they jumped to conclusions and presumed the worst – that she and the boy were having a sexual relationship. They were wrong. The young man was just an acquaintance. Nevertheless, my sister was banished from the house and shunned. This also meant her private school education ended.

My parents said she should be studying, not squandering the tuition by spending her time talking to boys. Mother resented the tuition money father was spending on that daughter.

My father and mother said she had to leave because they feared she would "set a bad example" for the remaining daughters at home. Father had raised his daughters with the hope of getting a good match through an arranged marriage. He wanted to have a voice in her choice and felt she was being disobedient.

At home, because this sister was shunned, we were not permitted to speak of her and we missed her terribly. We missed combing hair at night and having her shield us when we got scolded by mother. We missed her sharing her poems and drawings. We begged our dad to bring her back home and re-think his views. We felt this was unfair and our mother should have stuck up for her step-daughter.

Chapter 26: The Complexity of Dhoon and Rajdaye

There were some good, even great things, about my father. He had a multifaceted personality. He believed in protecting his daughters' virtue, and that finding each daughter a good husband was his most important role in life.

In those days for a man to have a vision, to let go of a permanent position such as a sugarcane-estate policeman, to become an independent businessman, took a lot of strength, foresight, and ambition.

Dhoon soon had his store stocked with dry goods, liquors, and all kinds of merchandise. We children waited on customers, restocked, and each was assigned exclusive responsibilities for store operation. He did quite well with the use of our cheap labor! It also gave us skills.

My father believed an education started the day a child was born. He wished he had garnered sufficient income to provide a higher education to all his children.

He was a complicated man. He had his faults: he had a nasty temper which resulted in domestic violence and he was a womanizer.

Having such a large, complex family was a great motivator for his ambition, or he may have felt trapped in what he wanted to achieve.

His strength was that by reading and educating himself, people looked up to him. He was a village elder. People admired him for leaving the small village of Corial, for buying the dry good store, with only few resources, for being able to organize and move all of us, so many people, to our own new location, and making a success of himself.

People looked up to him saying, "Well, you know, that man bought a dry goods store. How did he do it?"

If there was something going on in the village, he was asked to speak. When Mr. Dhoon gave a speech, people listened. When someone wanted advice, my dad was the voice of reason and logic. People saw him as a person of distinction.

Father's other kids didn't realize that my mother paid a heavy price for staying in the relationship with a man who already had a wife and children, and also for accepting responsibility for *ALL* his children.

Mother helped him by staying, by doing the cooking, cleaning, and laundry; by being a saleswoman in the shop, by being a construction laborer. She toiled from morning to night everyday.

All the while, when they weren't with us, she grieved for her first four children. My father's children helped my mom on household chores.

Father was verbally abusive and harassed her. He didn't want her to tell *his* kids what to do or to boss them around. Many times it was not what mother said, but how she said it.

Mother was always tired when we came home. I never

saw her relax at home, sit down to have a cup of tea, eat with the family, or even to rest. If she'd been yelled at, she relieved stress by yelling at us.

In the yard, we planted flowers where all of us said our prayers. Mother had us keep our altar clean. Many times, we found her praying aloud; at those times, no one dared to interrupt her, not even our father.

Everyday she asked God to come into her heart and to help her raise all the children. While facing the sun, she often prayed for patience and courage, and for people all over the world. She thanked God for the teachers, lawyers, the principal of our school, and most importantly, the taxi and schoolbus drivers who gave us a ride. We also heard her telling God about the need for money for our schooling. Her main grievance was our dad's behavior toward her. She told me, "Praying helps me cope."

We learned from our mother to pray, love God, and appreciate His blessings. Mother said, "Always do good, and good will follow you."

Mother became angry if her kids slept after sunrise; we marveled that her eyes changed color when she got angry from green to yellow. She'd lift up the bed covers to wake us up saying, "Don't let the day pass" . . . "Don't let laziness creep into your blood." . . . "Working people must get an early start!" She held us responsible for our chores to be done in a timely fashion.

She believed children should be seen not heard, and detested the fact that we sisters would giggle doing chores, fearing that meant we were not working. She put a stop to that by separating all of us during the washing, cooking, sweeping and ironing assignments. Mother ran the house like a drill sergeant, and she was often hated by the older kids for being the tough disciplinarian.

She didn't want any of us to stay up late – that meant after sunset. Mother said, "Nothing good comes after the dark."

We felt like she was a night watchman as well as our mother.

Her mantra was, "Always listen to our elders and show respect." She was so sharp she could anticipate all our needs. She worried about everything and everyone. She warned that she did not have any money to pay medical bills and expenses that would occur if we played rough and anyone got hurt. She took the words "personal responsibility" seriously and made us apply it to every aspect of our lives.

Everything was a teachable moment for mother. She groomed us to be good parents. She taught the girls housekeeping skills: cooking, cleaning, and ironing. She believed teaching these skills was her job as a parent.

Mother also gave advice to her boys. They were to learn all skills and how to run a small business, such as our shop. She wanted the boys to be self-sufficient so they could care for a wife and children later on in life.

My brothers took turns accompanying my father to the wholesalers, and on the ride, dad used the time to speak with them about the future and about making a living.

The boys had to weed the yard and chop wood for cooking. They had to finish their chores before they were allowed to swim in the river, or go to the athletic field to play soccer or cricket.

At times, they had to help us girls sweep, wash and iron. My brothers bonded with their sisters over chores, especially hanging the clothes on the clothes line and folding them. We had to be careful not to linger by the clothesline because mother was always watching to see who was wasting time and socializing. I always found time to talk and giggle. I was often the one distracting them with my stories and fantasies of becoming a movie star or writing for our newspaper. I was always getting in trouble with my mother for "skylarking," meaning goofing off.

My mother was extremely happy when we were doing homework for school, and these were also the times we could outsmart her and socialize. My brother Mike used to hide his comic book in his text book to read it. Whenever Mother found out, she burned his comic books, but he always found a way around her.

We were allowed to play with other children and go for walks, play hopscotch, cricket, soccer and "playing school." She dislike the idea of her children having friends. If they did, she went out of her way to get to know their parents, so she could keep a watchful eye on us.

However, mother forbade us to bring any friends home explaining, "We don't have enough food to give away because it will make us short the next day."

Mother was protective of the boys and warned them to be careful and not trust anyone. She was suspicious of people who wanted her kids to sleep over at their homes and cautioned all of us not to sleep anywhere but our home.

We were encouraged to attend prayer services at the temple. Mother kept a keep at a watchful eye on us there. I was always is trouble for talking too much.

One day the priest had my friend Vindra and I stand on the stage of the temple with our fingers on our lips because we had been giggling and talking during the prayers about the birth of lord Krishna. We were so humiliated we never talked unnecessary in the temple again.

Father wanted his sons to learn to play musical instruments on Sundays in the Hindu temple. When there was going to be a wedding, my father had his sons help in the village with setting the large wedding tent, cooking, cleaning and otherwise helping the wedding party. He wanted us to be ready for when our turn came.

We all grew up thinking we had too many rules and regulations, but our parents were preparing us for the authority of a workplace. As adults, we now see the value of the work ethic our parents instilled in us.

My father criticized my mother, complaining to us kids that she didn't like his other kids.

Our mother used the seven of us as pawns to get back at him. We were always in the middle between a rock and a hard place.

What would have helped would have been a place where mom could get out to visit her girlfriends, to talk to a therapist, to get help from a social worker, or other emotional support. Other step-mothers seemed to be better at finding such support and direction so that they could become more loving of their step-children.

From the time Dhoon and Rajdaye got together, it was a challenge to keep up with who was living where at any given time. In Ben Lomond, there were always his children and her children and their children coming and going. Someone had to keep track of it all: to supervise, feed, cloth, cook, transport, educate, discipline, groom, and look after them. It fell on Rajdaye's shoulders. When she sought the help of his older children in this way, Dhoon got angry and wouldn't let her tell them what to do.

For whatever reason, Dhoon never called Rajdaye by her given name. Sometimes he called her "Raj" or "Miss." When he was upset with her, he called her names (in the third person) such as "Number 10." Whenever he found her nagging his other kids, he'd call her "Crowbar" which made her crazy. When he was in a good mood, he'd say, "Hmm!" When he admired her beauty, he'd call her, "Lipstick."

Sometimes, she affectionately called him "Moon."

Dhoon detested that she had given birth to four children before she met him. It was a cultural thing. Most of the time, he kept his guard up around her. He thought showing her too much love might give her the upper hand. Dhoon and Rajdaye argued all the time, sometimes affectionately, but more often, it ended in violence against her. He yelled at my mom, called her names, and hit her frequently.

"How can you sleep with me, have children with me, love me, then hit me?" she asked.

When he hit her, she'd call out "Mr. Dhoon, Why are you hitting me?" She used this to call him back to reality.

When she argued with him, it was her habit to drag out everything that had ever been an issue between them. As a result, he called her "Joiner" because she joined together every negative memory before getting to the point of what needed to be resolved at that time.

Sometimes these pet names or derogatory names were like a code. They could be angry, or let off steam, but still let the other know he or she still cared. Other times, it escalated adding fuel to the fire, and resulted in Rajdaye being beaten by him. These were two good people that were caught up in a very bad situation of their own making.

My maternal grandparents' home was my refuge and I thank God for my Nanny Kasey and Grandpa Balkissoon.

Nanny Kasey cut sugarcane and carried buckets of water on her head down the road for the workers. She worked all her life to help support her 12 children. Nanny Kasey was an ambitious woman who believed in hardwork.

However, my Grandpa Balkissoon was known as a village drunk. This contributed to the Deen family's rejection of my mother. Unfortunately, alcohol was the downfall of several family members, and it hindered their ability to assist the family.

Their house was a sanctuary for us when we needed a safe place to go.

Our parents fought over the smallest of things. Mother took the beatings and abuse knowing we got what we needed because of it. Mother sacrificed for us, and didn't want us to notice what it cost her. Mike and I especially noticed, but our other siblings knew.

Father, on the other hand, was caught and torn between

two worlds. How could he see, and deal with, a mother who wanted progress for her daughters at home, when there was no mother to stand up for his daughters.

From his perspective, Rajdaye nagged and nagged. Dhoon used this as a justification to beat her into silence. But just as often, his remorse would prompt him to do whatever she'd asked.

His position was, "Look, I'll give it to you if you'll just shut up!" He claimed it was the only way to stop her accusations or criticism.

Mother felt if she didn't nag, she wasn't listened to. Unfortunately that was true. She got what she asked for but at a cost of being hurt physically and emotionally. She said she was not going to have another man in her life, no matter what. That's why she stuck it out, even when she was fed up.

I don't know if anybody else could have endured what she did in the daytime, and still compromise so much to be with Dhoon in the night. How did she do that? To some extent, she had to compartmentalize her roles as a mother: fending for her children during the day and being a being a willing partner to my father at night. She had too many children to become single again, plus nobody else wanted us, as we were so many. She couldn't face the stigma and hardship. She couldn't leave so she took it all.

To be fair, mother did try to leave several times, but those were to take a time-out to let him calm down. It was for her own and our safety; we always went back.

ða̵ ❦ ða̵

Our mother's sister, our Auntie Natasha stepped in to be the counselor for my parents. She stuck up for my mother and asked my father to behave. She will always be remembered fondly by all of us. She also took in Sarah at the age of 16 to help educate her.

ða̵ ❦ ða̵

To study at home was futile because of all the tension and quarrels. We were lucky we learned to read and write at all. While I could have given up easily, I kept on.

Neither my teachers nor classmates knew how much I cried going to and from school, and how many times I wanted to stay home because attending high school was an issue between my parents. This was because my father was upset that his other daughters did not get the opportunity or grades to attend high school.

Mom often said to me, "Your father doesn't want you to go to school because of *the other side*." That's what mother called Dhoon's other children.

It was difficult for us kids to be around the violence and strife. It made it hard to concentrate in school. When we were in school, we constantly worried about mother's safety.

I remember not being able to study or being able to understand what the teachers were saying because I was too worried about my mother. I was her protector and advocate from the age of four. I looked out for her. She was strong but emotionally fragile. After a fight, she wept uncontrollably. When she was upset, Mike and I went to help her as her comforters.

Living that life was emotionally scarring. Our neighbors knew when my parents fought because it would spill over into the yard outside.

After our parents had a noisy battle, the next time we went to school riding the bus, the other village kids whispered about our mother. It hurt to hear their remarks. We wanted to protect her.

When we told mother we were embarrassed to ride the bus, she said, "Some people have money, but no class."

Another time, when my brothers went to play football with guys at the field, they were the butt of ridicule.

In 1976, our parents had a really big fight. The villagers came outside to watch. Mother's head required stitches.

Father called Chandra's house "The Headquarters," and it fit. Frequently, while he was hitting her, he'd yell, "Take your orphanage and go! Get out of the house!" So we'd flee to the Headquarters."

It was our safe haven after father went into a rage, beat mother, and chased us out of the house. We always knew we could take refuge with Chandra and Dan at their house.

We are forever indebted to Chandra and Dan. We owe them our deepest gratitude. They were always there for us.

❧❀❧

Ben Lomond had fun things to do, too. One of our favorite pastimes was going to the drive-in movies with all the kids packed into our father's Austin Cambridge PF-2410 to see Hindi movies. Our father later bought a larger car, a Zyphr, which had two big horns, and he would toot that horn as he drove around town showing off. The villagers would come out to see the car. On the days father picked us up from school, it made us the envy of every child in school to see that car pull up to take us home. Sometimes he took all of us for Cannings ice cream. He couldn't afford individual ice cream cones so he would buy a gallon bucket, give each of us a wooden spoon and say, "Here. Dig in!"

We played hopscotch and other games. The boys played soccer and cricket. Our family had its own teams. Being a big family was a benefit in sports.

My three youngest brothers were born in 1972 (Anand), 1975 (Krishna) and in 1979 (Rishi).

Mike and his father Dhoon Ramlogan in 1981 when Mike enlisted in the Trinidad & Tobago Army. George is in the background (left). The building on the left is the house built for George.

Chapter 27: The Coalminers

We learned from each other where to run and hide after we did something wrong – places mother couldn't find us. There were times when mother would be looking for us because we didn't do our chores, or one child had hit another, or we had been sassy. Talking back was the worst offense.

That old shop (before the renovations) had wood plank floor, and slits in between the floor boards. The crawlspace was about 18 inches above the ground. Adults couldn't fit, but small children could.

Our shop sold dry goods, and served rum, Carib beer, Heineken malt liquor, and the like. That meant some patrons became tipsy and tended to lose dimes, nickels and quarters. Most dropped coins slipped through the cracks.

The previous proprietor, Mr. Jim, hadn't figured out how much money had fallen into those cracks. We kids figured it out fast!

The crawl space was also a wonderful place to hide. With a flashlight and a stick, we wiggled into the crawlspace between the bare ground and the floor of the store to retrieve any coins that had slipped between the slits in the store's wooden-plank floor. We always found something. This was one activity where it didn't matter which side of the family we were from. We little kids all went grubbing in the dirt under the floor.

If any one of us found a nickel, dime, or even a quarter, we were rich! Every once in a while, we'd find a bright shiny quarter or dime that was on top of the dirt. We knew then our dad purposely let the shiny new coin drop so we'd be sure to have a successful expedition.

Sometimes, we spent the found money to buy candy in our store. Several times when mother was angry because we were hiding there and refusing to come out. She tried to squeeze into the crawl space after us, but she couldn't, and she became stuck. We laughed at her because she couldn't catch us. That set her off. She'd throw something at us under the house.

When we were crawling under there with a flashlight, dad would ask, "What are you guys looking for?"

"We're mining. We are mining for money, Dad."

On the rare occasions when we found as much as a dollar in change, we would emerge from the crawl space covered in dirt and cigarette ashes, proudly holding the money in our hands.

We looked like coalminers!

When we grew taller and our heads hit the joists, we gave up going under the shop. Besides, we realized we were becoming easier targets for mom when she threw something under there.

Our three youngest brothers missed out on this adventure. By the time they came along, the old shop was torn down and rebuilt. They never experienced the joy of hunting for loot in the crawl space under the shop.

Chapter 28: Just One Egg

Mother brought my sister Sarah home for a visit one weekend while Sarah was on a break from middle school.

When I asked mother about Sarah being so fair and beautiful, she said, "God made her that way." She did not go into an explanation about Sarah and Molly's dad being lighter skinned or about their situation.

One day, Father had gone to the market to buy goods and returned with a few dozen eggs to sell in the shop. Mother took four eggs from the store and boiled them. She gave Sarah a whole egg. She cut up three eggs and divided them among 6 of us (Mike, Geeta, Parbate, Sugars, George, Curtis, and me). Warm and delicious!

The other kids must have squealed on mom. When my father discovered she had given an entire egg to Sarah but not the others, he became outraged. He argued it was wrong to take his eggs from the store and favor her daughter and not his kids.

Father insulted mother. Sarah began to cry. All the rest of us were crying for her.

This is just an example of how we had to watch mother suffer emotionally and physically. All mom wanted was to give Sarah an egg to welcome her back and show Sarah she was loved.

We all realized father's resentment was not only that Sarah was his step-child, because she reminded him of her biological father Deen. This was the inescapable conclusion because he loved Sarah's sister Molly as if she were his own child.

Father was so out of control that to buy peace, mother quickly packed Sarah's things and got a taxi to take her back to Gasparillo where she resided with her dad.

Mother's other children were all sobbing, waving good-bye to her. Father and his other kids stayed inside.

Hard-boiled eggs never tasted good again. Whenever I see an egg, I think of my sister.

Sarah Khan, a Muslim, and Seeta Begui, a Hindu, both Rajdaye's daughters.

Chapter 29: Earning the Privilege of an Education

Our parents decided Mike, Sugars and I would attend school. Some years we went in split shifts to make it possible. Mike and I were required to attend school mornings from 6 A.M. to 12 noon. Our half-sister Sugars went 12 P.M. to 6 P.M.

Since there was no cash to buy the third school uniform, to resolve this problem, Rajdaye walked from one end of the village to the other, seeking out people whose children had already graduated from the same secondary school. She begged for their child's old uniforms – whether or not the clothes were our sizes. Mother ripped open the seams, and altered the uniforms for us. However, father, not being able to sew, purchased new school uniforms for Sugars. He explained it by saying, "I know your mother is looking out for you and Mike, and altering uniforms for you, but I must look out for Sugars."

I was fortunate that villagers gave my mother the hand-me-downs for us. I had the wrong physical education uniform, and the wrong color shoes – with holes in them. I remember not having socks but I was happy to be attending middle school.

Mother also begged for used textbooks for Mike and me.

Mike and I attended Junior Secondary School until we were eligible for high school. We went to school by bus, and like most kids, came home to do chores.

As an older daughter, I fought for the right to go to

middle school and high school. Attending high school was a privilege not a right.

High School classmates Shanti (left), Latta (right), and Seeta (center) wearing their school uniforms. Note that Seeta does not own the regulation shoes. Her uniform is one that Rajdaye got second-hand and altered for her.

Chapter 30: The Abortion

A close relative died of a hemorrhage leaving two small children. Village gossip was, "She'd been pregnant. She and her sister came back from a trip to the other village, where she went to see a certain woman."

I persisted asking questions because I'd seen the bloodstains on her white burial sari. At first, I was shocked because I didn't understand, but later on I realized she'd had a back-street abortion. Her death played a significant role in forming my attitudes about life and the rights of women, in believing that even married couples should be able to plan the timing of their pregnancies. Her death made me wary about abortion. Sadly there was no sex-education advice for women in our village. It was a subject people didn't speak about.

That funeral was very sad. Older women were weeping. Rumor had it that financial difficulties caused the couple to want to terminate the pregnancy. The men were clumped together afterward giving each other advice. There were no secrets in our village.

Chapter 31: Train Tracks and Track-Houses in a Garden of Peas

In Ben Lomond, father noticed a tract of train-track land across the street from Mrs. Marahjin. He worked to clear that land, put a stake in the ground and planted peas. The pea plants grew rapidly and spread out and were used to reinforce a person's claim to land. Dad purchased Mrs. Marahjin's old property and made it possible for her to have a new place across the street. He acted as architect and general contractor to designed and build a house for Mrs. Marahjin. It was a handicapped-accessible house on one level to meet her needs. We helped her move in and get settled.

There was little in the way of planning and zoning in any jurisdiction or village in Trinidad. It was not unusual to find a big house here, and a small one next to it and across the street a series of shacks. Beyond the boundaries of the railroad land were fields of sugarcane. People who couldn't buy land knew they would never be able to own a house.

Another area up the street from us was called, "The Tracks." Although there were two sets of railroad train tracks, the trains no longer ran. These abandoned train tracks ran from Ben Lomond to Williamsville. Word got out that Ben

Lomond had prime real estate as track land. People flooded in to stake squatters's claims. People took advantage of the disuse to squat on the train lines and company-owned land. Actually, the Government owned the railroads, tracks, and the rights to the land on both sides of the tracks.

To start the clock on a squatter's rights on this railroad land only required putting up and living in a small residential structure. They could be built right up to the edge of the abandoned rails. We called them "line houses." Here each building was unique.

Most people felt it was complete when they hung up their hammock. It signified, "This is the place I live. It's where I can rest."

Dhoon Ramlogan (center) with his children Anand, Krishna on the bike, Seeta; and his granddaughters Guytree and Rohini on left and Geeta on her father's right in 1976 in front of George's workshop. Note the three appliances in front of the building awaiting repair.

Chapter 32: George's Property

By the time I was 14, mother and her step-son George couldn't get along anymore. Father built a detached shack for George and his appliance repair shop. It came about after George and mother got into a huge argument because the dust from his sanding was getting into our food.

In my child's view, I thought mom was just causing trouble and making herself a victim again. But this time she put her life on the line, so we could breathe clean air and eat food unadulterated by lead paint and other airborne pollutants such as asbestos which were a by product of brother George's occupation. We didn't know then that inhaling such dust and fumes from sanding and painting can cause pneumonia, lung and brain cancers, and birth defects. It is now known that lacquer and lacquer solvents can cause serious birth defects. Our mother may not have had the words for it, but she knew in her marrow that she had to protect her children from exposure to such contaminants.

My half-brother George resented Rajdaye and blamed her when his mother died when he was little. When she complained about the dust, George followed the abusive behavior of his father toward our mother. Father sided with George against Rajdaye on this issue and did not interfere with George's violence against her. This was not the fatherly or husbandly thing to do. Father was an elder, well-respected in the town, but in this instance, he showed seriously poor judgment. I'm sure it was based on the economics of the situation, instead of the parenting he could have exercised to control George.

George's business needed an air-filtration system, but we didn't have the funds or the knowledge of such things.

He and my mother fought over the issue of the dust from the appliance sanding in the garage, and mother got hurt and had to be taken to the hospital.

The values of male-controlled societies can really get skewed. Nevertheless, I am thankful the village elders spoke up for mother and gave her recognition for all she had done to take care of *all our father's children.*

The entire unfortunate episode with our mother made George grow up and he soon became a force for good and strength in the family. He became the go-to man.

Around 1978 when George was 19, he married a girl named Rupa from a good family, the daughter of a tailor. They lived in the house father had built him, which was set up with George's own workshop attached.

Unfortunately, George died in his 40s of a heart attack. He made peace with his step-mother Rajdaye before he passed.

Mother grieved deeply for George and we all realized how much she loved him.

Chapter 33: Years of Renovations

All of us worked in the shop after school so dad could make more money to build a better structure. In 1975, father demolished the shop to build a bigger one. He also tore down the residence attached to the shop, and with our help, he salvaged and recycled the reusable building materials.

Initially, we continued to live in the back of the building until he built a small temporary house next door on the land purchased from Mrs. Marahjin. Her old house was torn down and father put up a concrete structure for us.

A truckload of bricks were delivered and stacked in our front yard. When he laid the foundation and brick walls, Rajdaye acted as the hod carrier to bring the bricks and mortar to the place where the brick wall was being built. She also mixed sand, gravel, and water with cement to make the concrete.

For the new main structure behind the store, he poured a concrete slab and built four bedrooms on the first floor, and later added an upstairs.

To speed the process, dad hired contractors and carpenters to help build the residential part for us consisting of four bedrooms above the store and the new shop below at grade level. The new structure was larger, about 3,000 square feet with the store on the first floor and living quarters upstairs.

During the day, mother helped with the store and

residence renovations in the main building. In between running the shop, she labored along side the other construction workers. Her jobs were applying grout, mortaring, plastering, or smoothing concrete. She became extremely good at angles. Mother decided where the windows should go and helped install them. She sanded plaster. She worked construction, unpaid, for years while the house and shop were being built.

The store and living quarters eventually were equipped with kitchens, two bathrooms, two shower stalls, and the upstairs bathroom even had a bathtub! He installed cisterns to capture rain water so even when municipal water was unavailable, we had water for cooking, bathing and flushing toilets.

When the house was finished, we started Phase II: reconstructing the shop at the front of the building. By that time, we lived upstairs with the shop downstairs.

For two years, Mike worked as a water boy for an American contractor building public roads. As the full-time water boy he was paid well, even overtime. The job was not carrying drinking water to the other workers. Using a bucket, he had to bail standing water out of drainage ditches and the postholes, as much as 30-feet deep, so cement utility poles could be installed. Mike gave his paycheck to father to help finance the renovation. Whenever father needed extra money to pay carpenters, Mike worked overtime.

After two years, Mike had had enough. He enlisted in the Army. Like me, he chose not to have an arranged marriage.

After his 2-year military service, he traveled to India to study and became a Hindu priest. Eventually, he relocated to New York City where he is the spiritual leader of a large congregation.

Because we were only a year apart, Mike and I had been a team. In 1982, he immigrated to New York where he became a Hare Krishna priest. Even so, we've remained close.

Father was proud of that new shop!

When the construction was finished, he had no paint to dress out the interior, so for years, the shop perimeter remained the color of the exposed concrete.

To meet the customer's needs, he also sold cigarettes one at a time rather than by the pack or by the carton. Goods in our shop were often sold "on trust." The customer was expected to pay off their debt on the next payday. This credit arrangement also brought customers back to the store on paydays.

Dad restocked the shelves just before the sugarcane cutters' paydays.

During this time, the first word baby Anand spoke was "Overdraft!" Then baby Krishna's first words were "Credit" and "Wholesalers." Baby Rishi kept quiet until he could say, "Eat chicken."

As a result of several years building houses and renovating, father developed construction skills. When the economy was tight, he realized mother could tend the shop during the day while he worked for an American construction contractor on a six-month contract. He used the money for additional inventory and expanded services. He added tools, bicycle tires, inner tubes, and bicycle repair. In this way, he expanded the business. He branched off into a greater variety of products and services.

The Habbot Construction people liked father and gave him an Igloo water-cooler. We nicknamed it "the Habbot can." It widened all our horizons to believe that America was a place where an ordinary laborer could own a fancy water-cooler, one with a push button a worker could press and chilled drinking water came out. We thought it was fascinating.

Even now, the family still has the beloved Habbot can. At all the weddings and funerals, the Habbot can is present. It was an enduring symbol that the Americans loved dad.

Chapter 34: AA in Trinidad and Father's Inconsistencies

The life of the shop ordered the life of our home(s). For all of us, working in the shop was not optional, it was more of an order.

After children going to school departed in the morning, those staying home did chores and worked in the store. When we returned from school, the students took turns working in the store and doing chores.

Father's new shop flourished and he branched into selling bottled liquors. When the new shop was built, we had more room to serve customers seated at tables. Our shop had a drinking room with 8 to 10 tables. It became a political forum–sometimes we didn't even have room for all the people. They would drink and play cards.

Father's involvement with Alcoholic's Anonymous (AA) started because, before he met our mother, there was a period when he drank alcohol excessively. He sobered and went through the AA 12-step program. Because it helped him, he promoted AA and the 12-step program in Trinidad and made sure it was open to all races and ethnicities.

My father had dedicated his life to AA. This diluted the racial tensions that were a by-product of compartmentalized and tribal way of life. Alcoholism knows no race. My father would sometime take Rajdaye to AA meetings as there is a woman's group called Al-Anon. It was a rare opportunity for mother to dress up and be seen as father's other half. It was the only social outing she could enjoy with him.

Many sugarcane cutters, men and some women, budgeted a part of their pay for alcohol for ceremonial occasions such as weddings and social events, a custom leftover from the British. Rum shops, like British pubs, became centers for socializing and for political discussion. So father continued to sell alcohol in our shop.

We learned politics by watching and listening to all this. Teachers, lawyers, truck drivers, sugarcane cutters, from all walks of life, all races congregated in the same room to discuss political issues. Ours became a place for people to launch into politics. When people identified someone's truck outside, they'd come in to hear what the candidates had to say. It was a launchpad.

I also grew up watching men buy their rum, but not milk or shoes for their children.

Chapter 35: Sales Accounting & Survival

Rajdaye knew Dhoon was the proprietor of the shop; it was *his* shop. Whatever extras he could spare, he gave to his other kids.

There were days when my father bolted the door between the house and the shop to keep my mother out of the store so he could have some space. It was also his way to punish her whenever she had a quarrel with any of his children.

On the days when she was permitted in the shop, she sold goods. There she could stash money in a red cup, $10 or $15 from the day's cash sales and deposited that money in an account in her name at the bank. Her savings for a rainy day. Needless to say, father never knew mother did that. [Ironically that cash helped my parents buy land later on.]

On the days she was locked out of the store, there was no way to garner cash for the red cup.

When he found out she was dipping in the till, father assumed if she'd take money from the shop, she'd use it or give it to one of *her* first four children. She wasn't going to give it to any of us. Nevertheless, when she had to, she found a way to acquire what was needed, such as the cast-off school uniforms and textbooks. Most of their arguments were about the expense of sending kids to schools.

As time went by, we realized they no longer trusted each

other. But we also knew they still loved each other and were very attached to one another.

With Dhoon, she wasn't allowed to go to work for anyone else. There were too many kids at home to care for, and few adults in the extended family pitched in to help, as would have happened if their "arrangement" hadn't been so unique and strained. She rarely left the premises. She worked in the shop morning to night. She scrubbed the countertops, scrubbed the floors, and prepared the store before customers arrived.

When Dhoon wasn't around, she watched the shop, and weighed and packaged goods. In addition, she also had to cook, and Sugars helped her.

Sometimes he'd say, "I'll give you all something from the shop." We didn't take luxuries from the shop, only necessities.

Chapter 36: Graduation and Career Plans

Because I was a good student, my family allowed extra time for me to finish school before my parents arranged a marriage for me. I was 17 years old when I finished high school. I did exceedingly well with my final exams, especially in commerce, accounting, and Spanish.

I passed the career entrance exam. My goal was to work in the banking industry. Good job prospects were in sight for me, and I was accepted to work for the Royal Bank of Trinidad and Tobago in the capital, Port of Spain.

When the Letter of Acceptance came in the mail, my father immediately voiced opposition. "You are not going to be traveling back and forth from Ben Lomond to Port of Spain because there will be a lot of men, cars, transportation issues and getting home late. As a single girl, coming home late at night from Port of Spain will ruin your reputation.

"It doesn't matter what you say or what you want, you cannot accept this job. If you're going to find work outside the store, you must find something local."

With that, my father slammed shut my opportunity to enter the banking industry with a career position which would have opportunities for advancement and a substantial annual salary (not an hourly-wage worker).

I was unable to find suitable employment in Ben Lomond, so my next step was to look for work in the nearby but larger village of San Fernando. There, I was hired to be a Customer Service Representative. I was just a sales clerk in Nandlals' Variety Store. That was my first job outside the family business. With the experience working in my father's store, this felt like what I'd done all my life. Except for earning money, it wasn't a step up.

I soon discovered in the work place, there can be cliques, which can work for you or against you. For example, in this variety store, the Black girls in the store hung out together. The mixed-race girls of Indian and Black parentage socialized together as another clique. When I arrived, the exclusively Indian girls social network was already established. I realized I had to join the Indian girls because the others were even more exclusionary. People unfortunately form alliances and can have set opinions. I had to fit in.

After I got paid, my parents appreciated the benefits of my paycheck. Mother cashed it and gave me enough for carfare. The rest she used to buy necessities for my youngest brothers and sometimes something nice for herself. I loved helping her that way.

I had my hopes set on career advancement. However, in my parent's eyes, now that I was out of school, I was of an age to marry and have children. Mother was especially concerned since I was so rebellious and prone to making my own rules. She feared I might become involved with someone and have premarital sex. But she never discussed that with me.

Father bought us a 19-inch black-and-white TV, which we had to hit to keep the picture. He took the time to come out of the shop to join us whenever Indian dance music was televised. He'd playfully shake his hips and dance with us.

I knew there was a bigger universe that I wanted to be a part of. I wanted to experience a world outside of Ben Lomond. I aspired to be different, more Westernized. I dreamed of a new life for me in the United States.

It didn't matter if a girl had a plain face, if she had fair skin, she would be considered a better choice. Society made me feel *ugly* since my skin tone wasn't considered light enough and could prevent my parents from finding me a good husband. As the dark daughter, I didn't have expectations of getting married right away or at all.

Chapter 37: Without Warning, It was My Turn

Without warning, a suitor came forward and I was given my chance for an arranged marriage. One night, I overheard my parents having a serious discussion about a possible match for me to marry. I heard them say he was a young man of means, a good prospect. He was fond for me, a good prospect with a house, land, car, education, and a position as an engineer; but I didn't know this guy at all.

Soon my parents talked seriously to me about getting married, explaining the hardships of life and the sadness of not being married. I was supposed to accept what they told me for my own good. Without explaining what happens between a husband and wife in the privacy of marriage, they convinced me that marriage was the best idea. A daughter wasn't supposed to argue with her parents or elders.

Although we were in a the new house, my parents insisted on a lot of preparations — cleaning, new curtains, a new tablecloth — to impress the suitor's family when they visited.

Then my parents sat down with my brothers and sisters to let them know, "Somebody is coming to see Seeta."

My brothers and sisters teased me that I was going to get married.

My parents instructed me to wear my best sari outfit. At the appointed time, I was supposed to walk around the room in the traditional Indian attire in front of the guests so they could take a good look at me.

By this time, my dad had already checked out the family and made the decision that it could be a match. So when they came over to see my parents and me, it would be a serious discussion about blending the two families for the sake of the young couple.

The following day, a group of invited guests arrived and were seated in what passed for our parlor. Anand, Krishna and Rishi were young, so Ling and Geeta banished them to another room so they couldn't listen while such a serious discussion was taking place. Resentfully, in scarf, short silk top, bare midriff, and sari, I paraded around the room. The young gentleman, we shall here call Vijay, was seated along with his aunt, his mother, and other family members.

At a formal meal, the delegation discussed the possibility of an arranged marriage between Vijay and myself.

If the match were agreed to, there would follow a formal engagement period where the couple would be given several opportunities to have conversations to get to know each other better. After the dinner, the delegation departed. Vijay and I did not have any time to talk with each other.

I didn't expect him to like me because of my own insecurities and what I'd been told growing up. When I soon learned that Vijay said he liked me immediately and so did his family, I was surprised.

The next Sunday, mother and father weren't home.

Vijay came to the door. "I'm here to see your parents."

"For what?" I asked.

"I would like to set the date for the wedding."

"Whose wedding?"

"Ours."

My jaw dropped. "But I'm not gonna marry you! I never said I would."

"Why not? I'll take care of you – buy you a house, and take you to see cricket matches at the Oval . . ."

"I just said I'm not going to."

"Why?"

I had to find a reason quickly. I blurted out, "Because your ears are too big."

He looked shocked. "That isn't a reason not to marry! I'm an engineer and I own my own home. That ought to be enough. And I like you."

"Well, I don't like you."

"Your parents are going to be very upset," Vijay said.

"That's just too bad! I'm not going to follow tradition."

He asked, "What do you mean?"

"I'm going to America. So that's that."

"Going with who?"

"I don't know, but I'm going to America!" I blurted out. I couldn't believe my nerve! Hearing myself say that was a surprise, even to me, because I'd never thought seriously about actually relocating to America, only dreaming of going to America as a vague fantasy about a place I'd seen on TV. My reply had come out of nowhere, but I knew from TV I yearned to be in the United States. Not necessarily for freedom, but for opportunity. Like most Trinidadians, I believed if I could immigrate to the United States, I would have an opportunity for a better life. (Of course, until you get there, you have no idea how much work it is to live and stay there.)

The young man was so surprised he was unable to say anything. Waving my broom at him, I chased him across the yard. My gentleman caller saw he was defeated, and left.

Ling and Geeta looked at me like I was crazy. "What's the matter with you? You're taking matters into your own hands! You're making decisions that our parents should be making. You're going to be in big trouble," Geeta said.

I didn't want to see it that way. I wanted to make my own decisions and I didn't listen to them. I was more influenced by the West in what I was hearing and listening to.

Geeta added, "You're gonna get a good lickin' tonight."

"I am?" I raised my eyebrow.

"You're gonna get whipped."

"I'll run!" I said, feeling more brazen.

There was nothing wrong with how my parents arranged that marriage. What was wrong was that I chased that man away, and told him I didn't want anything to do with him.

Ling said, "Silly girl, Vijay didn't exactly come to see our parents or set the date for the wedding, he was here to talk to you and say that he liked you. If father had come home, then he could tell him that there was a match."

I was surprised.

When our parents came home, Geeta tattled. "That man

came by to see you about setting a date to marry Seeta, a date for the wedding. . . . You should have been here! Seeta chased him out of the yard with a broom!"

Father asked me, "Why don't you want to get married? And to such a good prospect?"

I realized how seriously father took his responsibility. Although we had some outside influences, our family was somewhat traditional. Without thinking about it, I said, "Why? Because I'm going to America."

Mother looked astounded! She called me every name in the book, then she turned on my father. "Dhoon, that girl is spoiled rotten! She's going to bring shame to the entire family!" Mother moaned, "Oh, how am I going to hold my head up in the village? Seeta's chased a suitor away. And she's not even good-looking – she's not even pretty. Bobbed-off hair. Look at her! She's so dark. She should be grateful any young man liked her at all!"

I never really saw myself like that, but they certainly did. They worried if I turned Vijay down, I would certainly end up a spinster, dependent on them, or worse.

"Dhoon, can you imagine it? He was such a good prospect! This dark Indian girl was offered a hand in marriage. An engineer! She insulted him, and turned down his offer. What are we going to do?" Mother gave me a beating for chasing away the suitor. I assumed I deserved it for disobeying my father and for being stubborn.

Mother had coached each of us for marriage. She often claimed I would bring shame on the family, projecting what she'd done and the shame she'd suffered. Now I know it was her way of saying "Don't repeat my mistakes."

Now I know my father handled my situation wisely. My parents knew what stage I was in better than I did. Although I knew all of this about our culture, and how much effort my parents had put into finding me a match, I still didn't want to be married at that time.

PART IV: SEETA'S DESTINY CHANGED

Chapter 38: Three Sisters Meet Mr. Motorbike

A week after I'd chased Vijay from our courtyard, it was a rainy August Sunday in 1981. My sisters Geeta and Ling were with me in our store when we heard a motorbike pull up and park.

A young man got off his motorcycle and came inside, "Do you have any coffee for sale?" he asked, looking at Geeta.

He has a nice bike; he has to pay for it somehow. He must have a good job. I'll speak to him. I pulled myself into the conversation. "Hello," I said.

"I'm looking for a cup of coffee."

"For what?" I said in a way to get his attention.

"I've been out in the rain and I'm cold."

"Well, I can warm you up." I was daring in the way I flirted, but I didn't know what that implied. Just something I'd heard on TV.

Under her breath, Geeta said, "Hot shot here reads too many Mills' and Boons' romance novels."

"I was just kidding." I said quickly. "We don't have any hot coffee, but we can get you a cup of hot tea or something."

He nodded.

I went to the back of the store to brew the tea.

While he was waiting, I overheard him boasting to my

sisters about his plans to go to America. I grabbed an enamel mug, poured the tea, and rushed to the front of the store, Pushing between my sisters, I said, "Move over! Move over! Let me hear what he has to say."

"My father lives in Tampa, Florida, and he has filed immigration papers to sponsor me to come to the United States." What he didn't say was his father had arranged a marriage for him that would be taking place in Florida after he had immigrated.

"Well, what's the keep back?" I asked, meaning 'What's the hold up?' I had a fleeting thought, *If this guy is going to America, maybe I can marry him and go, too.*

He changed the subject and asked, "Is this your father's store? Do you work here?"

Ling replied, "Geeta and I work in the store most of the time."

"I work in San Fernando," I offered, "in Nandlals' Variety Store."

"I'm a technician in San Fernando, too." He mentioned the address and he paid the tea tab. "Maybe I'll see you around . . . My friends call me 'Mr. Motorbike.' Thanks for the tea."

"Until we meet again," I said. "I'm Seeta Ramlogan."

Ling said, "This is my sister Geeta, and I'm Ling." She smiled sweetly.

After he departed, my sisters were excited. "Well, who do you think he likes?" Ling asked.

Geeta said, "Me! I think he looks as handsome as a movie

star."

I said, "No, me! I made him the cup of tea."

Geeta said, "If he's a technician in San Fernando, he has a skilled job."

"I work in San Fernando too," I said. *Can I look for an opportunity to catch his eye? Do I dare go behind my parents' back to talk to him? My parents can't think any worse of me. They already called me a ton of nasty names last week when I chased away Mr. Big Ears.*

I couldn't get the motorcycle guy out of my mind. In the middle of the week in San Fernando, I decided to check him out. On my lunch hour, I took a taxi to find his work address.

I found out he lied about being a technician. He wasn't!

He was a salesman in a small store. Before I could leave that store, Mr. Motorbike recognized me, "Oh, you're the girl in the Ramlogan's *big* shop."

"Sometimes. My day job is in a store near here."

"I hope you'll shop here again."

My heart fluttered. I smiled and excused myself to get back to work.

The following weekend, he showed up at my father's store when I happened to be taking my turn on floor duty.

He smiled when he handed me a gift of fruits called chennetts.

Over the next few weekends, Mr. Motorbike came by our store when I was conveniently in the shop.

For me, it became like a lifeline to hold onto. My parents

were already looking for other marriage prospects for me and were nagging me about getting married, so I knew with them it was only a matter of time.

I have to get out of here so I can help my brothers and sisters. If I go to America where the streets are paved with gold, I can send home lots of money to help with my three brothers and two sisters still at home.

August passed quickly as did September. My perceptive mother said, "You know, that boy is not a good match for you. You're an educated girl. I have misgivings about him."

My family did some investigating into his background. While they agreed he had some good qualities – a job, a motorcycle, a reputation as a good, kind person – my father wasn't thrilled about Mr. Motorbike. Dad wasn't comfortable with him as a prospect. Father became frantic to find another suitable match for me. I was becoming his problem child.

Mother, aware of her mistakes, didn't want me to make the same decisions. I was the daughter given an expensive education all the way to graduation and passed the O-level exams (equivalent to the U.S. Associates degree.)

On the other hand, she was a little nicer. I pulled her aside. "You know, Maw, if I get to go to America, I'll find a job and send you money for my sisters and brothers. I'll even send clothes and things for them. I'll be able to buy things for you, and to send home money."

She knew I'd be true to my word. I'd always given her my pay check. She was thinking that if I made it to America, I could help her more than if I stayed in Trinidad and married someone local. She became caught up in the dream, too, and looked forward to my departure.

The reality was that Mr. Motorbike had an entry-level sales clerk job, and he lived in a cramped apartment with his mother and sister while his mother worked more than full time to pay all the expenses for the three of them.

As the Ramlogans, we now had a nice big house, big store, a popular bar, and we were doing better.

My father was persistent. He went to Mr. Motorbike's current village to ask about him. He also went into the village where he had grown up. He learned that his family – the grandfather and the uncles – were decent people but his father, living in the U.S., had little opportunity for involvement with his children in Trinidad.

After six weeks, my father was still checking him out; all the while, Mr. Motorbike continued to come to my father's store to see me.

One day at work in San Fernando, I decided it would be fun to ride on Mr. Motorbike's motorcycle. I did not want my father to see us because I knew I would be in trouble for sitting so close to a man.

Somebody saw me riding with a boy on a motorbike and told my father. "That daughter of yours was straddled on a motorbike with her arms around a boy's waist. She must be just like her mother. That girl is going to bring shame to you."

They confronted me when I came home. "Is it true that you were riding on the back of that boy's motorbike – with your arms around his waist? Is this true?"

"Yeah, I took a little ride on the motorbike. I've never been on one before."

"Where did you go on his bike?"

"Just around town. Then, to see where his family lives."

My father and mother exchanged knowing glances. "What did you do there?"

"Nothing. I met his mother and his sister. We ate a little food, then I went back to work."

"Don't ever do it again!"

I looked at them funny. *What's the harm in getting a ride on a motorbike?*

From then on, I was labeled. "This defiant daughter who is giving us the most gray hair," mother lamented.

A week or two later, we went for another ride on his motorbike, and we stopped at his family's apartment again. This time his mother and sister were not at home.

I'd never been on a date. I'd never been kissed. No boy had ever touched me. My head was in a whirl. The apartment was hot. I guess we were too. One thing led to another, and before I even knew what was happening, we did the unthinkable! What we should not have done. Only a moment of passion. We had intercourse. Until then, I didn't know what that was and had never heard the word.

I was confused. I wasn't sure what had happened to me down there. *So it wasn't about riding the motorcycle after all. It was about eggplants and bananas*! At first, I wondered,

What was the big deal? It happened so fast. People make such a big deal about sex." I said aloud, "This is not for me, Lord. It's not for me." But for the first time in my life, I felt ashamed, ashamed of myself. I knew I had done something wrong. Not like someone telling me, "You should be ashamed of yourself!" *But How did I let myself do that? To think I did it with someone I'm not married to, and he doesn't even have a decent job. What was I thinking?*

I'd never had any physical contact with a boy. Not a hug, a kiss, or hands touching. I saw boys in class at school. But we were not allowed to be near one another. Not allowed to hold hands. Not allowed to kiss. Not allowed to give anyone a hug. We were allowed to flirt with our eyes, and my sisters and I did that a lot. We made eye contact with many boys. We didn't think it meant anything.

I was naive. I was inexperienced. Afterward I figured out that I now knew what my parents had been warning me not to do. I didn't realize that you could take off some clothes, and in a moment of passion, something significant could happen! So significant, your life would be changed forever. *I let this guy do this thing. Oh, my God! I just ruined my life!*

I've gone against everything mother taught me. I've gone against her. I've disappointed her and myself. How am I going to tell her? I know she will be upset, and I never wanted to disappoint her in my life. I always wanted to make her so happy and proud.

It never occurred to me not to tell her or talk to her. I was confused. I wanted to tell mother because I knew I'd done

135

something I didn't understand, but after doing it, intuitively, it felt wrong. Maybe she could help me sort it out.

Suddenly, I remembered mother's words. "If you have sex with a boy, you're going to get pregnant." Until that moment, I never thought she was talking to me, or even to my sisters. I'd always believed she was referring to her own life in the past.

After hearing those words echoing in my head, I worried. *Oh, my God – What if something happened? What am I gonna do? I'm not married. I don't have a real job. Would they throw me out like they threw out my sister?*

My siblings and I had watched how our mother suffered and had learned to cope and "settle" because she had so many children to take care of. She struggled for food and for money to send us to school. She wanted us to be careful, and to have the security and safety she didn't have. Mother especially wanted all her children to have an education, to read and write, experience learning as well as job training, so we could each make something of ourselves. All this raced through my mind.

A month of feeling nauseated passed and I kept quiet and tried to hide it from mom and dad.

Now, my hopes of going to America were dashed. Gone. I wasn't even thinking about America.

When Mr. Motorbike came back to our store, I said, "Listen. I don't want to see you anymore. I don't want to go with you to America and I don't like you enough to marry you. I don't want to marry anybody right now. I think I'll just wait for my father to get me a match." But really I was thinking, *Oh, Lord! Now I'm in more trouble than I bargained for – I should have married the guy with the big ears!*

I was sick and felt tired a lot. When I went home, mother looked at me funny, and she said, "You don't look right."

"I'm alright. I'm fine."

"When was the last time that you ate?" she asked.

"I was sick at lunch today."

Well, that was all I needed to say, that I threw up.

She called father in from the shop, and said in Hindi, "Dhoon, come upstairs as quick as you can." When he got upstairs, Rajdaye told him, "Seeta was sick at work today."

We had a big argument. In the course of the argument, I became aware that mother, who had always been our protector, before my eyes turned against me. I didn't like it.

Dad said, "I always knew you were going to do that. You should have married Vijay – the one you called, 'Big Ears.' You are bringing shame on us!" They went on an on and all the kids were listening.

I felt like I would be throwing up again.

It ended when father said, "Because I threw out my other daughter for far less than this, I am duty-bound to throw you out."

I ran for the bathroom.

Mother and dad had an ugly quarrel. He struck her because of his anger toward me. He yelled, "It's all your fault, Raj, for letting Seeta complete high school. There she became too Westernized, and forgot she was a Hindu girl. She should have been home washing dishes, cooking, cleaning, and being prepared for marriage."

When I came back into the room, I tried to protect her. I couldn't. This time, mother didn't defend me. She grabbed me by the hair, and pulled hard. "Come here!" she said. "Tell me exactly what happened."

I told her about the ride on his motorcycle.

"Not riding the motorcycle!" she said. "Did you *do* anything with him? Did you *have relations* with that boy? Did he touch you *down there*? Did he do *more* than that?"

"Yeah." I hung my head.

"Well, I think you're pregnant," mother said emphatically.

"I couldn't be! That couldn't happen." No one ever explained to me how babies are conceived or how to prevent it. They should have taught me all that stuff instead of talking about a wedding as security and staying off a motorcycle.

I was vomiting. In their eyes, any young woman throwing up in the morning, is definitely pregnant. It didn't matter, marriage was mandated. *No family members took me to a proper doctor to see if I was pregnant. There was no medical proof that I was actually pregnant.*

"We have to talk to him."

My parents and I went directly to the store where he worked in San Fernando. Father grabbed Mr. Motorbike by the collar and said firmly, "Get on your motorbike and come directly to our house. Our family needs to talk to you. Come to our house. Now!"

At our house, he defiantly revved his engine before parking his motorbike out front. He slowly climbed the stairs. Mr. Motorbike was shaking.

Inside, father looked him in the eyes and didn't mince words. "We think Seeta's pregnant. We know she had relations with you. You have to marry her."

Just like that!

Mr. Motorbike was so scared, he only said, "Sure."

To them, just admitting that you had sexual relations was enough. We had to marry.

He told me later that when my father took hold of him, at that moment, he saw America flash in front of his eyes, fade, and disappear, crushing his dream of being re-united with his father in Florida.

My husband's mother was in the United States making arrangements for him and his sister to immigrate to the U.S.A. By now, his mother had her own Green Card and she was arranging for Mr. Motorbike and his sister to travel to Florida.

Under the circumstances, Mr. Motorbike went to see his grandfather and uncles, and maternal aunts about having to have "a shotgun" wedding. He spoke to them because his parents were estranged, and both in the U.S.A. They feared marrying me would prevent him from going to the U.S.A. He promised to also file my immigration papers as soon as we were married.

In the meantime, my father sent a message to my sister Chandra, and another to the Hindu priest to come to our house right away. I heard my parents tell the priest I was "in a family way" so we couldn't have the full traditional Hindu ceremony.

The way the priest looked at me made me feel worthless and ashamed.

Then father sent a taxi driver to round up the other sisters and brothers and tell them "Get over here, we're going to have a wedding."

On such short notice, only a handful of relatives and friends showed up. Each asked, "Who is getting married? Why?" I heard my agitated father and mother loudly explaining to them, "Seeta has brought shame on the entire family. That's why we are having a wedding!"

Mr. Motorbike and I put on clean clothes, but I did not have the traditional three days of ritual beauty spa treatments. There was a make-shift altar with a few flowers, no tent, no village celebration. Everyone knew I was pregnant.

The Hindu priest performed an impromptu abbreviated Hindu marriage ceremony.

My sisters and brothers were crying, sorry I had to leave. My whole family was also upset that this turned out to be so embarrassing. They could never be proud of me again.

It diminished their dreams, too. The dream faded of having a foothold in America to work for the family's betterment in Trinidad. We knew I could and would help my family if I had the chance. The day I was married to Mr. Motorbike, all their dreams of Seeta helping any of them out of poverty evaporated. Now they felt I would never make it to

America.

After the ceremony, everything I owned was packed into the small black suitcase. I was sent away to live with Mr. Motorbike in his mother's apartment. My father told me to go stay there that night. It still hadn't sunk into my psyche that I was now Mr. Motorbike's wife and that a wife lived where her husband lived.

Then, I was told I couldn't go to work anymore because of the shame I had committed. I wanted to explore, to pursue even higher education, to grow, to have dreams and make plans. It was pulled out from under me, too. I didn't even know for sure if I was pregnant – a full month hadn't passed since he'd seduced me.

A few days later in the apartment, I suddenly realized this was now my destiny, my married life. I was to live in that apartment: married, sick, throwing up, and pregnant. Not the glamorous life in the U.S.A. I'd envisioned. Most crushing of all, I realized my life was not different from that of my parents. Maybe worse. Mother's marriage to Ram had been a legally arranged marriage with all the trimmings and community approval.

I was vomiting frequently. To make matters worse, the plumbing in the apartment was broken and the toilet would not flush.

Chapter 39: Simultaneous Weddings

My sister Sugars was taken out of high school to mind the store, and she was next in line for an arranged marriage.

In my opinion, Sugars should have been given the opportunity to go to high school, too. At 16, when Geeta wasn't doing well enough at school, our parents pulled her out of school to work. Although both Sugars and Geeta helped at home and in the store, they were still daughters – to be protected and provided for.

About that time, Geeta attended a cousin's wedding where a gentleman spotted her and subsequently fell in love with her. He was described as a nice man with a good job. His family visited father to ask if father would allow Geeta to join their family. At the request of the fiance's family, the Hindu priest set the date of the wedding and both bride and groom's families had to agree to the date, time, and place.

At the same time, a suitor had come forth for Sugars and father approved. His eldest daughter, acting in place of their deceased mother Jaya, made Sugar's wedding arrangements with the parents of the groom. Together my step-sister and the groom's family set the wedding date, time and place.

Father wanted them on the same day in the same place so the banquet afterward could be for both couples.

Unfortunately, it came about that Sugars wedding date was scheduled on the same date as Geeta's, but not in the same location. On the same day, both brides were to be married by priests officiating in the traditional Hindu rites at different homes far apart. Neither of these girls had finished high school, but they were obedient to our parents.

There are certain Hindu rites such as providing the dowry during the ceremony which were the responsibility of the father of the bride. Father was required to do this at both of the weddings.

When the schedule conflict came to light, the families were too reticent to approach either of the Hindu priests to ask to have the date(s) rescheduled. As Jaya's eldest daughter, Elsie had a lot of responsibility for her younger siblings and held firm that Sugars' marriage date should take precedence.

As religious people, the families feared asking for a change since that might be taken as a sign of disrespect. Worse, to ask for the date to be moved earlier might give the wrong impression, and so the families weren't able or willing to reschedule either wedding.

The ceremonies and arrangements posed logistics, pecking order, and geographical challenges, but somehow it worked out. It became a big deal deciding which family members would attend each wedding, and where and when to share the guests.

The result was father spent his energy running back and forth between the weddings, and watching his comings and going was as entertaining as the weddings.

જી ♥ જી

The following month, my sisters, brothers, and my father came to check on the newlyweds to see how we were doing. I was the only one home.

Mr. Motorbike's mother and sister treated me well and made me feel welcomed. However, when my family arrived at the apartment, they could tell right away I was unhappy.

"I'm very sad and I miss home," I said, tears streaming down my cheeks.

Dad looked around and said, "Okay. Pack up your things. We're gonna go back home."

Ling packed my things again into the same small black suitcase. My sister Ling and brothers were smiling, happy I was coming home. So was I.

At the same time, Ling confided in me, "When you got married, I felt as if the rug had been pulled out from under me. Here was our modern sister with the Farrah Fawcett hair style, who went all the way through school and graduated, who got to show off in the neighborhood, now reduced to a tiny black suitcase!"

I was crestfallen. My sister Ling always looked up to me, and made me feel good about myself. She did whatever it took to bring a smile to my face. She shared my dream of going to America.

After my things were packed, we all drove to find my bridegroom at his work. Father found him and said, "You can come to Ben Lomond to live with her. The place you are in is not suitable. Come to Ben Lomond when you get off work."

Chapter 40: Mr. Motorbike Became Unhinged

My parents gave us a bedroom in their house. They even set up a small kitchen for us so I could cook our meals upstairs. The family continued to cook downstairs.

An unintended consequence of our moving into my father's house was that (although I had daily commuted to San Fernando to work), Mr. Motorbike believed it was too far away for him to commute. A few days later, he lost his job.

The next day, mother looked directly at Mr. Motorbike and said, "We won't charge you for the room. While you live here, we expect you to help around the house, to help out in the store, and in general, to be part of the on-going construction downstairs where we're building an addition to the shop. On the days we pour concrete, you are to mix the cement with the sand and gravel and bring it to where it is needed. Other times, be helpful with whatever construction is in progress.

"Seeta, you continue to help with your sisters and brothers, to cook, to get kids ready for school, and help them with their lessons."

When we settled in, Mr. Motorbike wasn't comfortable with the schedule the rest of the household followed. Mr. Motorbike believed mornings were for sleeping. As always, Ramlogans were expected to be up early and ready for work to help with whatever Dhoon and Rajdaye needed.

When I'd awaken my husband, he would go right back to sleep. I woke him a few more times.

"Stop nagging me. I will wake up when I wake up. I am your husband. You don't tell me what to do."

"You don't understand. She wants you to make yourself useful and help around the house. Since you and I are living here, we must help to earn our keep. Mother is becoming angry."

With that, he got up, stomped around, and he did whatever she asked. He was not happy.

Saturday, same thing. He was sleeping late and mother was nagging me about him. She was carrying on about how I was pregnant, married, and back living under her roof where we had no right to be. She said, "You should be living with your husband and his people. You are was setting a bad example."

I guess she based this on her life when she wasn't allowed to move back home.

Where was the mother I knew as my defender?

She ranted and complained about how I brought him here, and she can't tolerate him because he is lazy.

At that point, my father stepped in. "Leave Seeta alone! I brought her back, and so it is okay for them to be here. Just leave her alone and let her be." *My father was defending me!*

When my husband was awakened, he heard all this and became enraged.

We had received a magnificent wardrobe with triple mirrors as a wedding gift. As it was being unloaded, Rajdaye raised her eyebrows and looked at the antique. She didn't have one as nice. She pointed out a problem with one of the mirror sections. "You have to fix this before the mirror breaks." Then several men laboriously helped Mr. Motorbike carry it upstairs to our living quarters.

The next time mother saw Mr. Motorbike, she turned on him. "There's something wrong with the hinges on one of the mirrors. Have you fixed it yet?!" mother demanded. "Repair it or pay to get it fixed. Get it done now, not later after the mirror breaks off. Take care of what you have." It wasn't what she said but how she said it.

He shrugged her off. His own mother never spoke to him harshly.

The next day, my mother insisted I wake him up to fix the bureau.

I did. "Listen–You really need to get up and fix the wardrobe and prove to her you are going to get it fixed today."

He became enraged in a way that gave him the strength of a silver-backed gorilla. He wrapped his arms around the dresser, dragged it to the backstairs, and shoved down all 18 steps, and put it in the backyard. He grabbed the stove's kerosene pot and poured the fuel on the magnificent dresser and set it alight with his cigarette lighter. *Boom!* The flame poofed up hot and stinky. The flames were magnified by the triple mirrors until they shattered. The finish bubbled, crackled, and melted as the wood burned.

At the smell of smoke, my father came bounding out of the shop, clearly distressed. "What the hell is going on?" Seeing the fire, he glared at Mr. Motorbike then ran to get water.

Neighbors were drawn to see if the house was afire. People flocked into our backyard – even neighbors from across the railroad tracks. Everyone was awestruck by seeing this fine furniture burning. People were speechless until someone said, "Rajdaye nagged him."

Understanding "Ums" and "Ohs," murmured through the group.

My sisters and brothers gawked at this strange man who set precious furniture afire. We couldn't save it. He burned it to the ground. Mr. Motorbike carried on like he was crazy. He called me every name in the book. "F..." this, and "F..." that, "You've ruined my life. I can't go to my father's place in America!"

I felt all faces glaring at me – the ugly duckling who had to get married. I was humiliated. *Oh, God! This is really shameful! Not only am I pregnant, but stuck with a hot-tempered man with no job–and now no bureau to put our clothes in!*

"What about me? I'm ruined, too. I can't go to America, either," I yelled.

Mr. Motorbike stomped past me, grabbed his clothes that had fallen onto the backstairs. No one tried to stop him as he wriggled past the crowd and took off on his motorbike. He didn't come back that night. He stayed away a few days, with his uncle.

When he came back, he said his uncle reminded him that his mother had taped her life's savings to the underside of the dresser drawer. He'd burned their inheritance.

Chapter 41: Mr. Motorbike's Immigration Papers

At two months into my pregnancy, Mr. Motorbike's papers came through so he could emigrate to the United States. My mood lifted when I realized, *Maybe it's not so bad – maybe I'll end up going to America after all.*

My father opened a letter that my husband received which indicated that the documentation for travel had finally come through.

Mr. Motorbike reacted unexpectedly."I don't have a clue what I'm supposed to do next. Right now, at this point, I don't want to go to America. You do. How am I going to pay for a plane ticket? Without income, we have a problem."

Seeing Mr. Motorbike was really upset, my father took him aside. "Son, you and your parents worked hard to give you the opportunity to go to the USA, don't blow it. This is your chance for a real life. I'll pay for the plane ticket."

His mother Jo had returned to the island and also urged him to emigrate to the USA. She was already anticipating his departure.

After my father and I gathered his required papers together, my father drove my husband to the American Embassy to collect his U.S. Permanent Residency Card, the document which would lead to getting a Green Card. The Green Card enables an person to live and work in the United States legally. After five years, a Green Card holder working in the United States could apply for U.S. Citizenship.

"Son, you get on a plane and go find your future for yourself, for Seeta and the baby!" my father said sternly.

In December, Mr. Motorbike left for the U.S.A. I remained in Trinidad and received a lot of love and attention from my parents, my wonderful brothers Anand, Krishna and Rishi, and my sister Ling.

I could not forget how my brothers asked the children in their schools for the milk and cookies they were not going to eat or drink and stuffed them in their backpacks and brought them home to me and my unborn child. This to me was the greatest act of love. Rishi was three at the time and he and I became very close.

In Trinidad in March, my husband's mother Jo suffered a stroke. I went directly into the ICU to see her and knew instantly she was dying.

When she saw me, she removed her necklace from around her neck and gave it to me. "This is all I have to give. This necklace is for the baby." A few seconds later, she took her last breath.

I was shocked. *Jo is dead, and her son's not here, and she just gave me the necklace, crying and telling me to take care.*

I knew the necklace was the only personal thing she owned. My father sent a Western Union telegram to Tampa, Florida to tell my father-in-law that his wife had died:

PLEASE SEND YOUR SON BACK TO TRINIDAD. AS HER ONLY SON, HE IS OBLIGATED TO PERFORM CERTAIN HINDU FUNERAL RITES TO BURY HIS MOTHER.

My husband came back to Trinidad in time to bury his mother. I was seven month's pregnant.

At the airport, my husband's way of greeting me was to say, "By the way, my name now is Don. Every immigrant in America gets a new name."

"Well, to me your are my husband and you are still Mr. Motorbike," I said

He pulled out his Passport and Green Card and threw them in the trash. "I won't be needing these. I'm not going back. I intend to stay in Trinidad."

Out of respect for his dead mother, I said nothing, but when his back was turned, I retrieved his Passport and Green Card and tucked them away for safekeeping. Although Mr. Motorbike claimed he no longer wanted to emigrate, I was still dreaming of America. We would find a way.

Our baby was born in June, 1982 and we named her Kimberly. It was Dhoon and Rajdaye's first biological grandchild. She was a beautiful baby.

Later when we talked about going back to America, my husband said he'd had a falling out with his father and didn't feel comfortable taking a baby and a wife to life with his father in America. He didn't want to be a burden, and money was always an issue, too.

My father arranged for Mr. Motorbike to work a construction job with a local large company. But I no longer felt a sense of security – not with my parents, and certainly not with a hot-tempered teenager as a husband.

When I got the chance, I told my story to my aunt and uncle who lived in Florida. We knew her as "Auntie Natasha" and appreciated her generosity; as students, she'd helped us get textbooks and school supplies. This time I wasn't asking for school supplies. I asked her to assist me in accomplishing my dream of immigrating to the U.S.A.

Auntie knew my husband's parents and extended family. She knew my husband had been called back home to Trinidad on short notice because of his mother's sudden death and the funeral.

"Please, if there is anything you can do, please help me, or help my husband by bringing him back to the United States," I pleaded. "Please," I begged.

"I don't know what we can do, but we will try to help."

Uncle Abraham agreed to fly to Trinidad, and after much persuasion, he brought my husband back to the United States.

As a condition of my joining him, my aunt, uncle, and mother insisted I leave my newborn behind to be looked after by my mother temporarily. My relatives also urged me to apply under the category of a Holiday Travel Visa.

I followed their advice and took a taxi at 3 o'clock in the morning for the two-hour drive through the mountains. At the American Embassy before sunrise, there was already a long line. As soon as the sun came out, it was hot. I was glad I left my baby at home with my mother.

At the window, the official demanded, "Where are you going?"

"I want to go America," I said. Then I added, "on vacation."

"Do you have family there?"

"Yes, my aunt and uncle, and my husband live in Miami.

"Why do you want to go to the United States?"

"I've heard that's the only country in the world where you can have an opportunity to make yourself somebody. . . . I've always wanted to go there. I believe in my heart it is the land of opportunity." I couldn't stop talking. I told him, "I watched *Farrah Fawcett*. I watched *Bionic Woman*, and I watched *Six-Million Dollar Man*, *Little House on the Prairie*, and *Frank Cannon*. I want to go over there and check it out for myself!"

You know what he said? "You're gonna go to America."

"I am?"

He smiled as he stamped my Passport.

When I looked at it, I saw it read, "Multiple Indefinite Travel Visa." This meant I could come and go to America whenever I wanted. That was the Visa my father said was nearly impossible to get!

I left the building elated. I hailed a taxi and slumped in

the back seat with a smile of satisfaction until I realized I'd agreed to leave my daughter with my mother.

About 10 minutes away from the embassy, I told the driver, "Turn around. Let's go back. The embassy closes at one o'clock. It's 10 minutes of one. Maybe we can get back there in time."

"For what?"

"Well, I want to get another Travel Visa."

"For who?"

"For my daughter."

"I thought you just told me you were going to leave her behind?"

"But what if I change my mind in the morning?"

There I knocked on the window again, but the window was closed. A man was standing close to an American flag. I asked him for help. "Can you help me find the same man who was in the window an hour ago? I must speak to him."

He left to find a staff member. He returned with the official. I thanked him and asked the official, "Can you please give me another Travel Visa, for my daughter?"

"For whom?"

"For my daughter. She's three months old. I'm not going to bring her on the vacation or anything this time, but I'd like it just in case I change my mind or can bring her next time."

"Well, you can bring her. You can bring her even if you are going on a vacation. It's free. You don't have to pay for a ticket for her either."

"I don't?"

He put stamps on the Passport, then took it into a back room.

I had a sinking feeling. *Oh, my! He might take away the Passport!* I was sweating. *I bet he's taking it away. I bet he's gonna – Why did I give him the Passport? What an ass I am! I gave away my Passport. I gave away my Travel Visa!*

Half an hour later, he came to the counter and handed me the Passport, Travel Visa, and documentation stamped for Kimberly and me.

At home, I told my father, "I got the Holiday Travel Visa, and I'm going."

"Well, okay," he said. "Now you have to purchase an airline ticket and make a reservation."

I bought my ticket for myself. Because my daughter was under two, she didn't require a ticket. I knew then I wasn't going to leave her behind especially since she could fly for free.

I recalled the pain of separation my mother went through with her first four kids. That separation and suffering would have been too painful for me. When I called my husband to tell him I had plane reservations, I kept quiet about Kimberly. Instead, I said, "We're going to follow through on the plan."

Mother assumed she had talked me out of bringing the baby.

At 5 o' clock in the morning, I was ready to leave. We had to depart in two hours. I almost changed my mind. Then I stuffed Kimberly's belongings into a black trashbag and brought her with me.

My father, my brothers, and sisters were sad to see Kimberly and me go. They especially liked baby Kim being in the house with them.

I was scared to death on my first flight to America. *Dear God, where am I going? I have no more money.*

I arrived in Miami that afternoon. The sky was blue. The grass was green. Everything was the same as in Trinidad, except it was hotter. *Where's the snow?*

My husband and Uncle Abraham picked me up at the airport. When they saw me with a small baby, my uncle was angry. "Why did you bring the kid?"

"Well, I couldn't leave her behind."

"What do you mean? Your mother was there. She said she'd take care of it. How are you going to go to school? How are you going to find a job? Who's going to take care of this kid, and who's going to take care of you? Your husband is flipping burgers for minimum wage and no benefits! Our home isn't set up for kids. A baby takes care and money!"

I was confused. *I thought in America no one had to work for anything and the streets were supposed to be paved with gold!*

I didn't see it from my uncle's view point, his American perspective. I didn't yet realize that in America you must pay your own way. In Trinidad where I thought I had it so bad, we never had to pay for utilities, rent, water and sewer, or even an electric bill. Coming to Miami was a big culture shock!

I later realized that to move from one country to another, you must plan ahead, and you must have money. It wasn't just an adventure. It was my life I was gambling with.

❦

Auntie Natasha and Uncle Abraham took us to their house where my husband, the baby, and I lived with them for at least a month. I was home alone with the baby. I cleaned and straightened the house and cooked. My husband's work schedule was erratic. My aunt and uncle also had day jobs.

I was too ignorant to realize it was costing my aunt and uncle to keep us. We didn't appreciate the hospitality they were extending to us.

Growing up one of 18 children, I'd never been alone at home before. I felt anxious and uncertain. I was in culture shock and homesick. When I was alone, I cried day and night. I wanted to go back to Trinidad. *The streets in America were not really paved with gold!* I was lonely, broke, and sad.

After a week or two, I began to panic. I couldn't go anywhere because I had no transportation, no spending money, and no babysitter. Without daycare for the baby, I couldn't even look for a job. I was raised not to believe in handouts. Our culture doesn't believe in handouts. I couldn't work. My husband had filed my papers to become a legal citizen, but it would take two years to come through. I was lonely and missed my brothers and sisters. In Trinidad we were poor in material things but we were rich in emotional support because we had each other there.

I felt better that my papers were filed. I was eager to help myself and help my family back home. Without the Green Card, I couldn't be hired, and I had no child care.

☙❦❧

I had no idea how we were going to survive. I was so homesick. Those were dark lonely days for me with no money, no job, and a husband who took out his frustrations by hitting me. I never thought I would be the victim of domestic violence, but I was stuck with him and the marriage, and felt I had to make it work. Thinking *If I just try harder....*

I also blamed myself for encouraging him to come back to the USA when he didn't really want to. At some point, I thought I deserved this punishment.

Chapter 42: The Distinguished Visitor

My aunt and uncle told us about an unfurnished house for rent in Liberty City. We would be responsible for the utilities, utility deposits, and furnishings, but we needed more than $300 to move there. We were still trying to figure out how to raise the money.

I got a job cleaning houses. Since I didn't have daycare arrangements, I took Kimberly with me to the job.

That week, one of my customers received a visitor to spend a week with them – a distinguished, older man who was wealthy and well-respected. After my boss left for her job, their guest approached me in the living room.

"Before she left, I overheard your conversation that you need money to move," he said. "Recently, I went to a strip club." He proceeded to tell me what he saw there when he'd watched naked women dance.

Then, he described how a girl could use her mouth to perform oral sex. "Do this and I'll give you 300 US dollars," he said.

I still didn't get it. "What does 'oral sex' mean? What

would I have to do for that money?" I'd never heard the words "oral sex" in my entire life!

He explained more graphically what he expected me to do.

He's really a dirty old man! I was flabbergasted. "You mean put my mouth on you. To eat that with my mouth?" I was shocked! "I'm not that kind of girl! I'm going to tell my father on you! This is not right!"

"No! Don't tell anyone!" he said, as he moved closer. By now, his private was aroused and he pulled it out to show me!

He touched himself more, moving his hand and pointed it at me. "Just eat it, baby. That's what I want," he said. "This is a generous offer!"

"You are a crazy man! Put that thing away!" *Oh, no!* I was scared. I was scared to death. *What can I do to save myself?* In desperation, I said, "I'll have you reported you to the authorities."

He laughed. "They won't believe you, you're an immigrant. Don't even bother." He pulled me close, rubbed against me, and I was terrified. I twisted and pulled away. I was a cleaning lady and needed to finish my work, but there was no where to run away from him. I had no car. I had no cash or credit cards. *I've got to get myself and my baby away from this man.* I backed up struggling to get away from him.

Suddenly calmer, I thought, *I'm still all right. I have a baby. I'll grab her and go into the study. I'll stay locked in there.* I grabbed my daughter, went into the study and locked the door. Isolated in the room, my mind was racing. I stayed locked in huddled on the floor until my boss came home.

She gave me and the baby a ride home to my aunt and uncle's place.

We moved soon after that, and I told that employer I'd moved too far away to continue working for her.

At home, I didn't tell Mr. Motorbike – he was a hot head with an uncontrollable temper. I did not tell my aunt and uncle right away because I was afraid of what they might do.

When I did tell my aunt sometime later, she was very sorry that stranger had made advances toward me at my job.

Now, I had a bigger problem to deal with. My husband was becoming progressively more violent. He was upset because the little money he was getting paid to flip burgers had to be spent on household expenses, baby expenses, security deposits for utilities, groceries, and rent, not the luxuries he felt entitled to buy. Added to this, we didn't yet own a car. My uncle let him borrow a car. We could barely make it.

Later, when I was back in Trinidad, I told my parents

about it. Mother wanted to ring his neck. My dad was furious. He said, "This was despicable. You should have reported him. He never should have done that! I am sorry I wasn't there to protect you."

Chapter 43: Adjusting to the Real U.S.A., Not the TV's Version

Trinidadians who came back from a visit to the United States often gave a false picture of what one can expect in the United States. "In America the streets are paved in gold! You should see the fast-food restaurants! Those French fries! You should see the big houses. They have air conditioning. Food prices are inexpensive. The roads, buildings, and bridges. You can pay for things with a piece of plastic."

But what people weren't telling you, was that everything comes with a price of hard work and sacrifice. Plastic credit card bills must be paid.

When Auntie and Uncle said they could put us up in Florida to help us get started. Auntie and Uncle were always there for us. Many times, they drove us on necessary personal trips and paid for the gasoline. They gave us a tremendous amount of help. We were too young to understand how generous they were with their time and their resources. They did that for me as well as for other cousins. They helped me become self-sufficient.

Chapter 44: Cleaning Lady

By now, I had a legal work permit, but no babysitter for Kimberly. I was still breastfeeding her. I needed to keep my promise to my mother to send her money and stuff she needed.

I handmade business cards and knocked on doors in a retirement condominium community where my aunt worked. I offered to clean condos for $5/hour if permitted to bring my daughter and let her sit in her stroller between shifts. I went to several houses a day.

My first customer was Mrs. Roslyn Miller. My first day on the job, with a smile, she handed me a small pail with 12 toothbrushes and a new pair of rubber gloves. "Here are your tools. Clean that!" Mrs. Miller pointed to the toilet and said, "Use these toothbrushes to clean the toilet. Be sure to clean around and under the rim."

In a matter of seconds, a million conflicting thoughts flashed through my mind. *Hell, no! I'm not cleaning this toilet with these damn brushes! Is this how I want my kids to remember me, on my hands and knees cleaning a toilet with a toothbrush?*

Then I snapped back to reality. *For $20 bucks, I'll do it!*

Mrs. Miller said, "Honey, don't forget to clean around that little knobs that covers the bolts. There's a saying in America, 'So clean, you scrubbed it with a toothbrush.'"

I nodded, but until then, I didn't think it applied to toilets. When she left the room, I pulled on the rubber gloves. Tears streamed down my face as I worked. *Oh! not me! Not in America! The Farrah Fawcett lady who paraded through the entire village in that short-short-skirt? . . . If I told my girlfriends back in Trinidad what I was doing in America, I'd be the laughing stock! I thought I had it so bad living at home, but we proudly hung our toothbrushes on the side of the house and used them only to brush our teeth! Toothbrushes are not toilet brushes!*

No one back home could imagine what I have had to go through in the U.S. to earn a living.

Mrs. Miller was a perfectionist, especially about cleaning toilets. On the good side, while I was working for her, she introduced me to the value of saving money for big things we needed, as well as having a "rainy-day fund" for emergencies.

Mrs. Miller continued to comment on my coming to work with substantial bruises. She sat me down and had a talk with me about the Cycle of Domestic Violence and what constituted abuse. While I denied it, she showed compassion and she knew what was going on. She felt sorry for me and urged me to get more education. She also gave me castoff items to send to my mother. I especially remember, she made me a tunafish sandwich on rye every Monday that I cleaned her house. Even though I'd just cleaned her toilet, she formally set the table and used these occasions to teach me table manners. In addition to my hourly rate, she gave me an extra 50-cents for busfare.

I still love tuna on rye sandwiches.

Mrs. Miller recommended me to her friends, neighbors, and bridge club and I was able to get more customers in her complex.

Chapter 45: Hitching a Ride

As time went by, Mr. Motorbike and I arranged our shifts so that one of us was with our daughter. As the baby got older and needed to move around more, I met an elderly lady named Nene who was able babysit for us.

Eventually I raised my rates and was cleaning houses for $20.00 each, clearing $200/week while my husband was only making $75.00 a week.

I went to the Mall to buy what I could afford for my daughter's first Christmas. I bought her a beautiful hat and dress. I was excited to get home to wrap it for her Christmas.

After shopping I went to the bus stop, and the bus was pulling out – I'd missed it. I would have to wait another 45 minutes for the next one or take a taxi and spend $10 instead of the 50 cent bus fare. Or I could save my money by walking home. Which ever option, I'd be late and have to pay the sitter more. There were no payphones in the area where I could call the babysitter to tell her I'd be an hour and a half late because I'd missed the bus.

Back home, it was typical to ask for a ride.

Just then, I noticed a tall man in a station wagon looking at me. He'd seen me run for the bus that just left. He was a white guy with sandy-brown hair, and a space between his front teeth – I'll never forget his face. He offered me a ride.

I did the unthinkable. I said, "Would you be so kind to chase the bus for me?"

He agreed.

Stupid me, what bad judgment I had. I got in his car. Once seated in the passenger seat, I realized this was a horrible mistake because he power-locked the doors.

I must get out of this car and go wait for my bus.

The man refused to stop to let me out. Then, he made a U-turn! He was no longer following the bus route home!

"Why are you going in this direction? The bus is in front of us."

"We aren't going there."

Oh, my God! I was scared.

He took a route that went over the railroad tracks and onto the West Dixie Highway. He glared at me and his left hand was fingering the power lock control.

He drove to a remote public park and stopped the car in front of a public bathroom. He unbuckled his pant's belt.

"What are you doing, sir?"

He got out of the car, came around to my door unzipping his pants. He demanded, "Come out of the car."

I have to make a run for it. This guy is too dangerous. I stepped out the car, ducked past him and ran. I had to abandon my purse with my $20, my Passport, keys, all my wallet pictures, along with the bag with Kimberly's new Christmas outfit.

Thank God, I'm wearing tennis shoes! I'm not rich enough to own high-heeled shoes, thank God. I spotted a park security guard. However, with no Identification or Passport to show, I was afraid to ask for help.

The guard looked at me kindly as I passed him but I didn't dare stop. I ran, and ran, and ran!

Somehow I got home.

From that experience, I learned not to put my life in danger to save the 50-cents bus fare.

Chapter 46: No Safe Place

At home, my husband had paid the sitter. He was angry that I'd been out longer than expected. I was disheveled and it was dark out. I was afraid to tell him.

He didn't ask me, but he went into his typical rant blaming me for everything bad that had happened to him.

Not being able to tell about the incident, or be reassured by him, caused something to change in me. *Why was I staying in this marriage when I was now able to earn my own money, as little as it was*. But this time, I knew I needed a plan.

At that time in the USA, if you wanted to work, there were plenty of jobs. I encouraged my husband to go back to school, or to get a GED. I suggested he could sign up for an adult education program to get a certificate and a career path. He took it as nagging and got violent. I usually got hurt. Like my mother, I didn't know when to keep quiet. We both needed counseling.

Throughout my marriage to Mr. Motorbike, the physical, emotional and mental abuse never stopped. He put me down by saying things such as: "You are dark and ugly . . . Nobody would want to be your friend. . . . You are stupid. . . . Uneducated . . . You had no business coming to America."

I had it in my mind that, *Once we own home, he will be happy . . . Once he has a place for his things, he will be fine.*

Then Mr. Motorbike will stop hitting me. I worked hard to
make a better life for us and make him happy but the violence
never stopped.

My bringing up his getting a GED to him felt as if I was
saying he was inadequate as a man. This was twisted thinking
but it let him blame me whenever the topic came up. Any
suggestions he took as nagging.

Chapter 47: Immigration & Naturalization

My father never knew how many struggles and challenges I faced in those first two years. I didn't tell him I was cleaning houses for a living. I only told mother about the dirty old man at my employer's place, but kept quiet about the other time when I missed the bus and was almost raped.

Needless to say, they didn't know I was being abused by my husband at home, or had to ride three buses to work. Back then, in Trinidad, an Indian woman would rarely ride a public bus alone.

I had made a promise to my mother I would help her and that kept me dreaming and seeking opportunities. In life, it's how you present yourself. I believed in the power of lipstick, eyeliner, and a big smile. I didn't complain about my life. I wanted to present myself to my family in a good way.

America meant so much more to my father after I'd immigrated. At first, he was sad because he had lost me. My brother Mike was traveling finding himself, and the family was shrinking in that house – only some daughters and the three youngest boys were still at home.

My father recognized the potential benefit of my American dream for the entire family. He saw my being in

America in a different light – as a supply chain of tangible goods and as an inspiration for my siblings.

I bought a Polaroid camera. I took a lot of photographs in America and each time I went home to see the family. I remember my father's face when I took the first Polaroid picture of him. He watched the photo materialize. "Oh! it's me! I can't believe it, but I'm right there in the picture. How did you do that?"

I explained it to him, and he was so pleased with me.

When I gave father a butterfly-type paperclip to clip together his papers in the shop, or gave him an actual clipboard, he was so impressed and proud! His own clipboard! It represented a miracle as well as a new status for him.

In his store, we saved empty gallon bottles similar to the plastic milk jugs used in the U.S.A. He'd carefully cut an empty container in half to make a scoop and a funnel. One time, I brought him a real funnel for dispensing cooking oil, and big scoops in assorted sizes for packaging rice and flour. These were among the tangible benefits to him from my being in the U.S.A.

I never knew how much he loved it until years later when Ling asked me, "Did you realize every time you sent him something from America, whether mailed, shipped or hand carried to him, he'd show it off to everybody?"

"Yes."

Ling said, "He showed off the T-shirts, socks, shoes, the big scoops, the funnel, the case for his eyeglasses, the clipboard, even the paperclips. He boasted about it all! He told all the customers, 'My daughter Seeta sent this *for me.* These things were Made In America!'"

For me, the important thing was to send something that filled a need.

No one else in the family had a camera or a video camcorder. Later, I discovered disposable cameras. The family treasured the gifts I'd sent them.

My joy and satisfaction was in sending things back to my family, but it became a major problem in my marriage. With so many people at home, and not being there to help, I felt it was my duty to help from afar in whatever way I could. I'd made a promise to my mother and Aunt Natasha that I would do that.

Mr. Motorbike detested the fact that I was taking money I earned, and once in a while money from the household account, to buy things to send home to *my family.* He didn't understand the need for me to help my family. From his standpoint, I was being unreasonable.

For example, after the shop had electricity, I bought a typewriter for the store and a sewing machine for Ling.

After they had built the big house, Anand, Krishna and Rishi would hear the noise of torrential rain falling loudly against the metal roof because there was no ceiling to their bedroom, only the roof rafters. The room was open from floor to the underside of the roof.

I sent money for installation of proper ceilings for each room so they would not be open like boxes. It felt more private to have a room with all its surfaces. I paid for four ceiling fans, too.

Ling let me know father was proud of the ceiling fans. He couldn't stop raving about how he could now turn on any fan with a wall switch, not a cord. "Seeta, the little things you did made such a big difference to the family back here," Ling said.

I yearned for approval from my mom and dad.

I cleaned houses until two weeks before giving birth to my son Michael in 1984. My husband called him "our Indian Prince" when he was born.

When I came home from the hospital, we had an argument because the other new mother in my hospital room had flowers from her husband. I asked Mr. Motorbike, "Where were my flowers?"

He had a loaf of bread in his hand and threw it at me, hitting our Indian Prince instead. Luckily, the baby just smiled.

In 1985 that I had to go to Port of Spain to pick up my Permanent Residency documents that permitted me to live and continue to work in the United States. Because all my papers were legal from the get go, the United States required me to go back to my country of birth to re-enter with the legal documents. Illegal aliens entering the United States skip this step.

I went to Ben Lomond to see my family. I'd been away two years. Mother said, "Your father is no longer a violent man. Things are better now. We only have the three boys at home now and we are concentrating on paying for their educations."

I had loaded our suitcases with shoes, sandals, pens, pencils, spiral notebooks, and other items made in the U.S.A. I packed M&Ms, Crayons and coloring books, products people in the U.S.A. take for granted. On this trip, I brought my family simple things, like Q-Tips, clothing, and cottonballs – little things that I could stuff into a suitcase.

Family members were proud to have things marked "Made in the U.S.A." When the kids received the surprises, they were elated, especially about the T-shirts, something unfamiliar to them.

There was no question in my mind that fate played a hand in my life. I was fortunate to have met my first husband when I did. Had I not, I would have been married to Vijay or some other man of my parent's choosing. Although Vijay would have made a good husband, it is unlikely I would have had the opportunity to come to the U.S.A. where I eventually became a U.S. citizen.

After my husband, our children, and I spent two great weeks in Trinidad, we had to get back to work in the U.S.

Four carloads of my family came to the airport with us to wish us bon voyage. It was a happy and sad time for me. My extended family didn't want us to leave, fearing that we would never have enough money to come back to see them ever again.

My husband had his suitcases packed with Hindi videotapes and cassettes of Hindi music. These were very important to him — his priority.

At the airport, when American Airlines announced that our flight would be departing one hour early, we didn't hear it. Surrounded by so many family members, we did not hear the announcement. An hour later, when we went to the gate, we were told the flight had left an hour ago.

There, my family was on the other side of the gate watching us and waiving goodbye. Soon it was apparent to them there was a problem.

Mr. Motorbike got angry and yelled, "It's your fault we'd missed the plane because you were talking so much with your family and they are so loud." He was screaming. "My Hindi films are on that plane with the checked baggage but we aren't with them." He chased me through the airport and much worse. He even took away my passport and immigration documents.

A crowd was gathering around us in the airport. People shouted, "Leave the girl along!"

My brother Anand jumped the rope, grabbed Mr. Motorbike and pulled me away from him.

The children were crying. We were stunned and

embarrassed. I wanted the earth to open and swallow me.

Father intervened and spoke to the agent, who told him our baggage and the Hindi films would be held in Miami and that we should return the next day at the same time.

Mother was crying that she didn't want the children and I to go to America with him. She said, "He's bad luck. Don't go with him!" Even my sisters were saying the same thing.

We went home to my father's house in separate cars. Mr. Motorbike stayed overnight at Chandra's house. The family spoke to each of us separately about getting along. Mr. Motorbike expressed his remorse for hitting me claiming he couldn't control himself.

I told my father, "I'm sure I want to go back to America. I worked too hard to get my Green Card, I don't want to give up now."

My father replied, "If you go back to the U.S.A., you have to make a future for yourself with or without him. If you leave him, you have my blessing. I would support your decision."

The next morning, I was bruised and banged up. My father drove all four of us while lecturing Mr. Motorbike, "Never lay a hand on my daughter again."

I forgave him, the father of my children, and wanted a fresh start in America.

Chapter 48: Mrs. Newman said, "Stop, Run, and Go to School"

After returning to Miami, I met Mrs. Florence Newman in the hospital when I was working as a home health aide for a temp agency and Mr. Motorbike was working in an auto-body shop. At first she didn't like me. She said I was too skinny to be lifting her. But she soon realized I was very competent.

When she was discharged from the hospital, she needed 24-hour care because of her frequent falls. So the agency assigned four home-health-aide's to her care, and I was fortunate to be her caregiver.

During my time with her, she noticed my bruises and asked me about it. She finally blew up at me and said, "Stop, run, and get an education. You don't deserve to be hit. You don't have to take it."

"But my mother did."

"This is America. Don't stand for it. You can do better. You are a leader not a follower. Get an education for a job in demand. Do this for your own kids, not just your mother's kids!"

She became my friend and a life-changing mentor.

Mrs. Newman said, "It's unconscionable that your husband would hit you. You need to get an education and move out."

It may sound funny, but until Mrs. Newman said it, it hadn't occurred to me that there could be any way out of domestic violence. My mother hadn't found a way out.

Mrs. Newman gave me advice emphatically. She said, "Our lives are constantly evolving. This happens one day. The next day, something else. Don't cry over the past. Are you going to cry your entire life? You can't. You must make a plan, and move on. You have to take care of yourself."

In the meantime, my husband and I had saved enough to make a down-payment on a three-bedroom, two-bath home in Hollywood, Florida. Our employers provided proof of employment and we obtained an FHA home loan. After we closed on the house, it was the first time I'd ever seen Mr. Motorbike truly happy. He took an interest in fixing up the home.

When my husband phoned me at work, Mrs. Newman overheard my side of the conversation, defending myself about why I was working, and thinking about going back to school. She could even hear him shouting into the phone and using bad language to put me down. She wanted to protect me from him. She said, "Do not teach your children that staying under the tyranny of domestic violence is acceptable."

She saw something in me that I didn't realize I had. She saw leadership. She always said to me, "You have leadership qualities. You're very ambitious. Use that ambition to make a safer life for yourself."

Mrs. Newman showed me the way. "Make a plan. Get an education with job training specific to a career, get a secure good-paying job. Chart your own direction. Don't stop after you graduate. Always set goals and plan ahead. Continue to read, work, and chart your own course. You don't have to depend on a man to have a life."

I realized that I enjoyed being with the elderly, working in the hospital and in their homes as a nursing assistant. It was a joy even when it was hard. It came naturally. It was my calling. This is the direction I should focus on my education: nursing. I realized there was a demand for nurses to do eldercare, especially in nursing homes.

Mrs. Newman kept nudging me to stop talking about going back to school. "Do it already," she said. "Plan ahead for your future and that of your kids. But for God's sake, put the plan into action!" Her encouragement inspired me to speak to a counselor at the community college.

She reminded me of my mother. Mother had instilled in me the value of an education. In America, I understood it even more. I learned it is important to have training and education to be able to get ahead.

The counselor explained the difference between loans, grants, and scholarships and made it possible for me to apply for a grant to finance part of my education. Until that moment, I'd only known about working your way through school or night school. When you are working and going to school, it's difficult, and more so when you are a parent with small children.

I had a new resolve to find a career path, where jobs were in demand and in a field I would enjoy. I needed to go to back to school to get specific training for a career. That is when I decided to become a nurse. I continued to work as a nurse's assistant while in school to become a Licensed Practical Nurse (LPN).

I paid for a babysitter when my husband was at work and my husband watched the children in the evenings. I missed spending more time with my children, but I knew in this way, I could give them a better life. I struggled for those two years to succeed in school – an abusive husband, little cash, two children, sharing a car, but I had a dream.

He was so against my ambitions that one semester, in a fit of rage, he ripped up my expensive textbooks. I was so humiliated in front of our children. He was jealous and thought I was doing too much to make my parents proud of me when he wasn't. He felt as if he were being pushed aside. That I was moving on and leaving him behind. This became his self-fulfilling prophesy.

Mrs. Miller, Mrs. Newman and other employers also taught me social graces, American table manners, appropriate fashion sense, and how to go about getting a college education in the U.S. What I wasn't learning in the classroom, I was learning from them – American history, social mores and norms, respectful conversations, and how to live. I was always open to constructive criticism and got life skills from these wise women.

Most importantly, Mrs. Miller and Mrs. Newman taught me about the Cycle of Domestic Violence. After hurting a woman, a man will become affectionate and want to be intimate, unfortunately that doesn't mean the hitting, derision, and rage won't happen again, and become increasingly worse. I began to see the bigger picture. Mrs. Newman pointed out that abuse includes name calling, being choked, pushing, shoving, threats to kill, hair pulling, accusations, berating, screaming and yelling, broken bones, as well as power and control issues such as demanding sex before one could go out, trying to prevent one from going somewhere, demanding sex when one came home because she'd been out. It's not unusual for an abusive husband to forget what he has done in a fit of rage. Such "selective amnesia" makes it easier for the man to deny what he did in his anger. Domestic abuse was commonplace back home and too common in America as well.

❧❧❧

Mrs. Newman had numerous follow-up medical appointments. When her sisters Virginia Hirsch and Rose Schwartz could not take her to her doctor's appointments, I became the designated driver. Mrs. Newman was not accustomed to a simple life and was amazed when taking rides in my Chevette with no air conditioning and holes in the seatcovers. She sat in the passenger seat, holding her cane, well-dressed, not a hair out of place. She predicted that one day I would own a car with air conditioning and no holes in the upholstery. She normally rewarded me for taking her to the doctor's appointments by taking me out to eat.

She used these occasions to teach me about her people, her culture, and her love for the state of Israel, New York City especially Central Park, and the U.S.A. in general. She shared her memories of the struggles of her family during the time of the Holocaust. Her love for her sisters was amazing.

I had the privilege of meeting her sisters, especially around the Jewish high holy days. They taught me how to make Matzo pancakes, Matzo ball soup, brisket. They made me feel wanted, welcomed, and beautiful.

She also told me stories of her world travels and her work with the Izod clothing company.

I learned a lot from her and how to be strong and confident. At the age of 22, she insisted that as soon as I could afford it, I buy good life insurance for my children, get health insurance for all of us, and a disability policy. She taught me about stocks and bonds and how the stock market works.

As a Hindu girl and an immigrant to the U.S.A., I was most influenced by Mrs. Newman, a kind Jewish lady. She encouraged me, was my mentor and a friend. She made a difference. I was with her when she died.

Two years later, I obtained certification as a Licensed Practical Nurse (LPN). My father was proud when I graduated. I called him when I started my first LPN job, where I was making more than $12 an hour.

Dad was elated. "More than twelve U.S. Dollars an hour?" He couldn't believe it. "That's a lot of money!"

I liked working because I could help so many people. I promised to send one day's salary each month to my parents.

Mr. Motorbike saw that as being disloyal, as a betrayal. He believed *our* earning belonged to us for *our* household and *all* the money should go into one pot for the household expenses. At the time, I didn't understand that. I felt obligated to use my earnings to send money and things home and keep my promise. I never saw my earnings as belonging to our household here in America.

One of my solutions was that, as a team, we should both earn more money. Another was *If Mr. Motorbike would watch the kids on the weekends, I could work then, too.*

He was okay with it. It gave him time on the weekends to watch more Hindi videos at home while taking care of the kids. He was extremely good with the kids. He enjoyed cooking, dancing to the Hindi music, reading stories, and playing with them.

Soon I was working one job Monday through Thursday for a 12-hour shift, then got the kids from the babysitter, went home and took care of them; and on Friday, Saturday, Sunday, I'd work another nursing home job from 7 A.M. to 3 P.M., and he took care of the kids on the weekends. During the week, the kids were in daycare from 6:45 A.M. until he picked them up at 6:45 P.M.

Chapter 49: Few Regrets

When I met Mr. Motorbike, it was not love at first sight, but I grew to love him. We planned a life as a family. There was no question in my mind that I wanted my marriage to be successful. This is what we were conditioned for as Hindus. "Stay married no matter what comes your way" is drilled into every young Hindu.

Had it not been for his temper and violence, I would have remained married. We would have worked out our differences. However, I knew what a life of domestic abuse would be like and I wanted no part of it.

It is difficult to get over the pain from someone you love who betrays trust.

When an abuser hits a person in anger, the physical force is full of venom and can be deadly. For me as a wife, living with Mr. Motorbike was like living with a time bomb that could explode at any moment.

I felt helpless. At times, I did not even want to breathe for fear of breathing the wrong way and setting him off.

He hit me all over. I took all of it because at the time I could not do better. Suddenly, I understood, in a new way, why mother stressed that a woman needs an education. A woman must be able to make her own money and have options. She must be able to protect herself, and to protect and provide for her children, regardless the state of the marriage.

Of all the daughters, I was the daughter whose marriage was dominated by domestic violence. Mr. Motorbike would not control his temper.

I place some blame on the environment in which he was raised. He claimed all women should be subservient and domestic as depicted in the Bollywood films (Hindi-language movies). Even so, his own mother worked to support him. Mostly he had a lot of growing up to do and so did I.

I paid a price for not listening to my parents and for defiantly choosing my own husband. We were married for seven long years. Trapped in the cycle of violence, I kept believing that each beating would be the last. He was usually nice to me afterward, so I wanted to believe it would not happen again. How could it?

We even agreed to avoid confrontations. But the strain and the violence took its toll, and I fell out of love with him.

I was blessed to have two wonderful children from this marriage and I thank God for them.

Anyone considering immigration should be aware that you really shouldn't immigrate unless you have somebody at your destination to help you, and you have some place to live. Have a wise person explain to you about the costs of shelter, rent, utilities, security deposits, mortgage payments, housing finance loans, school loans, tuition and textbooks, dormitory fees, groceries, taxes and insurance, automobile license, automobile license exam, automobile insurance, minimum wage, payroll tax, income tax, property tax, building codes, health codes, as well as how many unrelated persons can live under the same roof in that jurisdiction, and much more.

You don't go to America to sit in an easy chair and watch wealth pile up. You have to work very hard here and make big adjustments, but it can be done. You need to have a plan and mentors along the way.

Chapter 50: Seeta's Divorce and Newfound Freedom

Becoming a Licensed Practical Nurse and working two jobs caused problems for me at home because Mr. Motorbike felt like he was no longer in control. He claimed, "You've become too independent."

I liked the independence and felt safe at work. I was growing away from him. I needed to be away from him because it was so distressing being put down and hit. I also enjoyed earning money and the confidence that the increase in pay from being a nurse afforded me. I'd found my niche. The nursing homes needed workers, and I enjoyed the patients. I learned a lot from their wisdom and experience.

As a child, the cycle of violence I saw in my home led me to believe that all women who are able-bodied must have a job, or an independent income. Women especially must have their own money. At times, it is a woman's only way to get to safety and protect her children.

Mr. Motorbike got upset when I spoke to people, if I had any friends, if I wanted to go to the grocery store by myself, or if I wanted to phone home. He wanted to isolate and control me; the only way he knew how was through violence.

At any time for any reason, I could to be hit again. Throughout the seven years of our marriage, I took his rages and being hit because that was the culture in which I had been raised. It was expected that a wife would stay put.

I would have benefitted from counseling as well.

I also wanted to prove to my parents that I had a successful love marriage, not an arranged marriage. I painted a too rosy picture for them of our marriage and our life in America.

His temper was so volatile, he could switch from charming to violent in a split second. After getting hit so hard that it left scars, it was clear I must no longer stay with him. I must not put up with that any longer.

In the beginning, I thought it was my fault. Did I say something? Should I have kept quiet? Then I'd try to make it up to him by apologizing, when in fact he was the one hitting me, shouting and carrying on.

Accepting my fate was what I had learned from my mother. She took the blows time and time again. Even when she got away from him to a safe place, she always went back to my father. I thought I had to, too. She taught me that children should have a mother and a father sharing the same house, no matter what.

I mistakenly believed that if I could have predicted when he was going to blow up, I could have protected myself. But it escalated anyway.

One day we had a visitor, a divorced lady named Pamela. My husband feared she was giving me tips on how to get a divorce. The reality was she needed a ride to work and it was not out of my way to drop her off.

While I was drinking tea with my friend Pam, he picked up a bottle and smashed it on the kitchen floor to scare her away. He yelled, "It's not proper for you to be hanging out with a single woman."

I was embarrassed. I made up my mind I was not going to take it anymore. Mr. Motorbike left to take the children to school.

Pam had been a battered wife. She whispered, "Out of every bad situation, good can emerge. Your future can be bright."

My jobs increased in responsibility as a Charge Nurse and a Team Leader. I became more self-assured and my self-esteem grew. After a life of being put down for being dark and told I was ugly and unlovable, my patients and their families, the medical staff, my staff gave me confidence that I was an attractive competent intelligent person. This was what I needed. As I grew at work, I became increasingly frustrated with the situation and tension at home.

There were two Seetas: the one who was ambitious and flying through her new career and finding successes; and the put down Seeta who was walking on egg-shells at home. The

Seeta at home couldn't wait for dawn so the successful Seeta could get back to work where it was safe and productive.

Once my mind was made up, I got restless to get on with the divorce. Sometimes to survive, you have to leave whatever situation you are in to get a fresh start. I didn't want to fall into a man-dependent trap the way my mother did, getting in so deep I could never get out. Or staying, no matter how many beatings. I'd watched my mother's suffering trapped in the cycle of violence with no education and so many children to provide for she couldn't leave my father. Something had to give. I knew I was in a trap, too, but I decided to get out. For me, the marriage was over.

After I made the decision to end my marriage with my husband, I was emotionally drained, but still went to work at the nursing homes, because I had to pay the bills and babysitter.

I knew I had to provide a future for my two children. I wanted them to have an education which included attending college.

My mother's words came back to me: "Get an education, get a better job, and get a life!" My mother firmly believed she was mistreated by my dad because she lacked an education. As a child, I saw this violence, and I vowed no longer to be dependent on anyone.

After my children's father and I separated, the children

and I remained in the same house and he lived elsewhere.

ва̤ё̤ва̤

I believe every time you stop a loss it is a gain.

Although the court ordered Mr. Motorbike to pay child support, he never did, and I never asked for it because I wanted him to get on his own two feet and be there when my children needed his love.

In this case, I lost child support but I gained my freedom.

ва̤ё̤ва̤

When mother learned I was getting a divorce, she suggested she could come live with me and watch my children when I was at work. It seemed like a good idea. I was also eager to show mother all the wonderful parks, restaurants, and shopping malls I'd discovered in Florida.

It was an eye-opener for my mother. But she was not accustomed to having unstructured time. I treasured the time my mom was in the United States. She was a big help to us and she and I became very close.

ва̤ё̤ва̤

In the meantime, my sister Ling and my father tended to the shop and children. Ling became their mother and father, because father was becoming mysteriously absent from the store at odd hours day and night.

While mother was still visiting me, based on letters from Trinidad, it did not take long for Rajdaye to figure out that Dhoon was having another affair.

PART V: FINDING MY SOULMATE

Soulmates Ahmad and Seeta Begui. Ahmad is holding the business card for the urgent care clinic he opened in Rockledge, Florida.

Chapter 51: Ahmad Begui

Sometime after my divorce was final, at the nursing care facility where I worked, I met a medical student named Ahmad Begui. He was divorced and his ex-wife had custody of their son, BJ (Ahmad, Jr.).

Ahmad was such a kind, considerate, highly-educated and handsome man that I fell head over heels in love with him.

One day, Ahmad was fishing for a date and asked about my schedule.

"I work here at this nursing home Monday through Thursday 7 A.M. to 7 P.M. On Friday, Saturday, and Sunday, I work at another nursing home. On those days, I get off at three o'clock, which is good for my kids."

He shook his head. "I can't believe how many hours you are working every week. Over 70 hours a week!" he said. "No woman should ever work that much. That's inhumane. I have never heard of such a thing."

Knowing how many hours my mother worked, I wondered, *What planet is he from?*

After I got home and thought about our conversation, I decided that guy's a keeper.

In the months we dated, I learned what it meant to be truly courted. Ahmed left candies in my parked car. He slipped love letters through my open car window. We went on many dates, our favorite restaurant being IHOP. Most importantly, he loved and cared for my two children Kimberly and Michael, as well as his own son BJ. Our children played well and quickly became friends.

We dated for four months. Then he told me he had accepted a residency in emergency medicine at Cook County General in Chicago and he was expected to report there for work within 60 days.

I was torn up when he told me he was leaving, but soon elated when he proposed to me AND my children, inviting us to move to Chicago with him. He even proposed to take financial responsibility for all of us. I discussed it with my children, and their father while I considered his offer. Their father was pleased we were not asking for child support.

In a phone call to us, my father questioned me that Ahmad was not of our Hindu faith and an immigrant from the Middle East. He was concerned about how we would blend religions and cultures. Ahmad took the phone and assured my father that religion would not interfere with our children or our lives.

Before I could accept the marriage proposal, I had to make arrangements for my mother who was staying with me. It was decided she would stay with her sister. Her sister, my Auntie Natasha, would find her a job as a housekeeper so mother could send money home for the children.

We also set up the visitation schedule and arrangements with Mr. Motorbike to see his children.

As soon as these arrangements were put in place, I accepted his proposal of marriage. Suddenly, there was a whirlwind of activity.

Mother was thrilled I was given this opportunity to start afresh with a kindly nonviolent man. She was proud I'd found a good match who got along with our big family and tried to make her happy. She was especially proud I was marrying a doctor and believed it gave her status as well.

Then she ruined it by saying, "I never thought that dark-skinned Seeta would end up with such a handsome, intelligent man!" She paused before kidding me, "Seets, you have the best luck! Do anything he asks you to do including scrubbing his feet everyday[1] – but always make your own living, just in case."

Coming from humble beginnings as I have, I appreciate whatever we have achieved all the more. For us, hardwork, dedication, and sacrifice has paid off.

My husband says what God gives with one hand, he can take back with the other hand, so you have to be careful what you do with what you are given.

I have come to realize that religion is a way of life. Your relationship with God is personal, sacred, and individual. I

---

[1] "Scrubbing his feet" was a reference to the story of Queen Seeta, a Hindu deity, who scrubbed the feet of her husband King Ram each day, then kissed his toes lovingly.

am a proud Hindu who believes in the power, blessings, and compassion of lord Krishna.

ॐ

Ahmad and I planned our wedding in seven days. We were in love and making a new beginning. I felt like the luckiest woman in the world who had found her prince charming.

I had to pack up my home, find a suitable renter for my house, and drive cross country. We caravanned from Hollywood, Florida, to Oaklawn, Illinois, even before we had a place to stay in Chicago in 1990.

We stayed in a motel for a week until we found a two-bedroom apartment in a lovely neighborhood. While Ahmad was at the hospital working, I went to nursing homes to look for work. I found one that hired me on the spot even though they said they had no job openings. I started work the next morning, even before we were moved into our new residence.

I chose to continue working because I enjoyed it and I liked the money. I also felt it was important to support my children so that we would not be totally dependant on my new husband. I'd learned from my mother, a woman needed an independent source of income. I remembered my mother's advice, "Never give up making an honest shilling."

Missing my mother, I phoned her everyday. I felt guilty leaving her behind. But just starting out, we could not yet afford to bring her.

In Chicago, even though we were married, Ahmad showered me with love and attention, and lavished me with gifts, dinners, and trips. He was proud of me and showed affection for my children.

My fondest memory of Chicago is of being on the Oprah Winfrey Show twice. One TV show was about being a maid, and the other was about hasty marriages. I was in the audience and was chosen to answer Oprah's questions. I thrilled to meet the talk-show queen.

Ahmad's residency lasted three years. In 1991 toward the end of my third pregnancy, Ahmad's 11-year-old son, BJ came to live with us. Ahmad, Sr., was thrilled BJ could be under his roof. Kimberly and Mike now had a step-brother coming to our household. Two weeks later, our daughter Jasmine was born. Our family was growing exponentially.

Like my mother's, my family was made up of his, mine, and ours – with all the challenges and sacrifices of a blended family. I was grateful I had grown up in a household where I learned so much about step-parenting dos and don'ts. It was not easy in the beginning for each of us to accept the other's children. We learned from my parent's mistakes a better way to love all the children. It also helped that I contributed financially to cover the expenses of my children.

Ahmad introduced me to Persian art, rich culture, ancient civilization, cuisine, and literature, especially the poets Rumi and Hafez. Persians take pride in their parenting, supporting the family, education, gardening, and cooking. The women are beautiful, kind, outgoing and love to dance.

⋅⋅⋆♥⋆⋅⋅

After Ahmad finished his residency, we relocated to Marion, Indiana, where we bought a house. It was a loving, supportive family-oriented community and we made many close friends. There, I only worked two days a week and loved being a-stay-at-home mom for two years.

During this time, mother came to Indiana and lived with us for more than a year. She and I took many road trips between Marion and Chicago. On these long drives, she had the opportunity to open up about the highs and lows in her life, her love for children and the three men in her life, and the times in her life which seemed most unfair.

Mother confided that she was married off to a man who did not come to love her, fell in love with a man of a different religion who did not stand by her after his family intervened, and afterward was smitten by Dhoon who promised to protect her and loot out for her. She said she remained with Dhoon because of her love for him and for all of us even though she was mistreated.

We grew closer as she shared these stories of her life – and she advised me about mine (whether I wanted the advice or not!)

She loved going to Chinese restaurants and walking in the malls. In downtown Chicago, I took her sightseeing and we rode on the elevated train with Jasmine. We went on the tour bus to the Field museum and the Art Institute. This was a precious time, one of the few where I saw my mother enjoying life.

I assured her that in her older years, we would all take care of her and never judge her.

While in Indiana, my mother watched *The Lion King* and *Alladin* movies with Jasmine over 100 times. She spread her attention equally among Mike, BJ, Kimberly, and Jasmine.

If Kimberly or Michael brought home friends, mother would remind me that "Their friends must be checked out first, because they may influence our kids to do wrong things." She cautioned me that, "Once a stick is bent, it is hard to straighten it."

Sometimes mother's teachings caused a culture clash because my children were Americans. They needed their friends here.

In mother's view, a child must be respectful at all times and not be insubordinate to elders. She believed in spanking children when necessary to teach them right from wrong.

When her visit ended, mother returned to Trinidad to assist Dhoon in finding suitable mates for the four youngest children, now of marriageable ages. Ahmad, the children and I moved to Satellite Beach, Florida. Kimberly and Michael were happy to be in Florida so they could see their dad more often.

Ling, Chandra, Molly, Krishna & Sharon, Seeta, Sarah, and Geeta on the occasion of Krishna and Sharon's wedding.

Chapter 52: 'No Fury Like a Woman Scorned'

After Rajdaye returned home, she confirmed what she'd already learned from a letter sent her by a sister – that while she was working in the U.S.A., Dhoon was seeing another woman!

Rajdaye suffered emotionally. My mother was made to endure the very pain and suffering that she had unwittingly inflicted on my father's first wife, Jaya. She endured that very same pain for the same reason – my father had taken a mistress. Our mother suffered deeply at the betrayal.

We couldn't understand it, but she still loved him. However, by that point, she couldn't cope with Dhoon stepping out every night.

Rajdaye's sister said, "I have had enough of listening to the family woes, knowing Dhoon was cheating on your mother. I said to her, 'Rajdaye, ain't no woman going to make you suffer no more. You suffered enough for ten *genim*! Ten lifetimes!'"

Rajdaye and one of her sisters went to see the mistress. Raj said to her, "This man has 14 children and four step-children. Right now he has four children at home. Is that what you want? Eighteen children – it's not easy. Do you want my place? Do you know how hard it is to keep that many people happy all at the same time?"

When my father found out Rajdaye and her sister had confronted his mistress, he was furious! I could also see in his rage a kind of sneaky admiration: *So here it is – Rajdaye still loves me enough to fight for me!*

Dhoon loved Rajdaye and they had their moments, but I think by then he was in love with his new mistress, too. He told one of the kids, "The lady attends to my needs quietly without all Rajdaye's drama and inside-and-outside-kids' commotion."

Chapter 53: Dhoon Ramlogan Died in 1993

The night before Ling's wedding, when all the grandchildren and their parents were sitting, visiting, playing, and hanging out, Nanny could not stand it. "Why are all of you wasting time? Get busy!" She scattered everyone, giving all of us chores. She managed to take the joy of out relaxing and visiting – what we call "liming" – by calling it "doing nothing."

My father smiled at her and shook his head. We all understood and loved that she was just being herself.

Whenever Rajdaye believed her life would get better, something else happened. . . . A month later, when mother thought her troubles with Dhoon were resolved, my father suffered a heart attack. My mother and George got him into the car to take him to the ER. Even while suffering a heart attack, on the ride to the hospital, father completed my brother Anand Ramlogan's scholarship application documents and had them stop at a mailbox to drop the documents in the mail. It was the last act of his life. He was DOA by the time they reached the hospital.

My father also spent time with my three children and was proud to see baby Jasmine get her first tooth on her visit with him in Trinidad. It was also Jasmine's first birthday. As the family gathered around her, my father showed her how to blow out the candle.

On that visit, my father asked me to buy him new prescription eye glasses. I realized I would move heaven and earth for him because I loved him so much. I made sure he got the glasses.

After Dhoon's death, mother had to cover substantial debt. Dhoon left no savings or life insurance. She had to support the three youngest boys at various stages in school. That year, the shop made enough net profit only for basic necessities.

Anand was in law school with a scholarship to go to the University in London. Krishna was studying to be an accountant in Trinidad.

Later, Krishna used his skills to take care of the book-keeping and accounts payable for the store. Krishna also helped to provide for 16-year-old Rishi's secondary schooling, textbooks, clothing and expenses.

After he was gone, we all recognized what our father had done for us. He had instilled a strong work ethic and leader-ship qualities. There was also a sense of regret for all he did to my mother. We knew his love for his children was great, but we also knew that, as his outside family, we could not compete with the others. Father had faults and I am sad he did not live to see the successes all of us achieved. He would have been proud.

Thankfully, my father had lived to see his youngest daughter Ling married. The best wedding ever in the family!

At the funeral and afterwards at the cremation site, a lot was said. The funeral pyre was built outside on land, and set afire. It took three hours for the conflagration to thoroughly burn to ash. As we waited to scatter the ashes on the nearby creek, all his descendants sat in clumps on the hillside, separated by the traditional family factions without any mixing and mingling. By custom, Rajdaye was not permitted to attend Dhoon's cremation.

My father's brothers and sisters ignored the factionalism and used the opportunity to have a talk with us. My uncle said, "That due to culture and religion, as children you were ostracized as 'the outside children' because your parents weren't married and Dhoon already had a legal wife and children when he met your mother."

This conversation should have taken place with us when my father was alive. I felt so good after they spoke to us.

Sixteen brothers and sisters were there along with at least 12 aunts and uncles and many villagers. Lots of issues were worked through while waiting for his body to complete cremation.

I asked my father's sister, "Why was it that so many people in Corial had come to my mother's defense, while his own brothers and sisters kept quiet."

She apologized and invited us to visit her in Canada. She was proud of us and now opened lines of communication for us. That opened the door for the other family members to chat with us.

My uncle helped us understand that the attitude wasn't just within our Ramlogan family, it was an island-wide cultural thing.

"Why didn't you treat us right when we were little?" I wanted to know.

One of my father's brothers said, "Our society wouldn't permit it. Your father went against all custom being with your mother, and your mother went against all custom coming to live near him in Corial village.

"Your mother and father were crazy about each other. Your mother understood the situation by the time she moved to Corial. After Jaya died, your mother was unprepared to take care of such a blended family. Just like your father found it difficult to love her first four children, Rajdaye found it a challenge to love and accept his other seven children. This is what caused the rift.

"Nevertheless, she was determined to make a life and a living with your dad. And he took responsibility for each of you from day one.

"His parents did not agree with him, but he went against them because he loved your mother."

Father's sister nodded in agreement.

Another uncle reminded us of the saying, "Don't laugh at what others are experiencing just because you haven't felt it. What hasn't met you, probably hasn't passed your way yet, but it may."

My father's brothers and sisters were deeply moved that my mother had taught us the importance of forgiveness, and we held no ill-will toward them.

Through her tears, my sister Molly said, "Dhoon treated me so well I felt as I was his own daughter.

ია🐦ია

When father's ashes had been scattered, it took away a lot of hurt and bad feeling, leaving a more peaceful atmosphere. It didn't take a conflict resolution negotiator or a psychiatrist to do it, just people with common sense talking honestly on a hillside.

ია🐦ია

My father died with some measure of peace. Mother still loved him even unto death. He died being in love with a mistress – a crushingly terrible blow to our mother. My mother was a jealous and proud woman who loved Dhoon with all her heart. Behind all the bickering, after the kids fell asleep, their romance and passion endured; it produced seven children.

The day after the funeral, I spent time with my mother. I expected to find her weeping. Instead she seemed serene.

"Mother, how can you be so calm just one day after father's cremation?"

"I loved your father very much. I always will. I know he loved me in his way."

"We all loved him, ma. He was a good dad," I said.

Rajdaye continued, "But now I'm free. Now my life is dedicated to all my children and grandchildren."

"Yes, this is a beginning for you. All your child-rearing duties are behind you. You and father together had combined, a family of 18 children. The children are grown up now. You have a nice house and the economic security of the shop. You can have any life you make for yourself. It will be good."

"Yes. Now my love can no longer cause me misery. I did my duty. I raised my kids and his kids as best I could. I helped in every way necessary," mother said. "The remaining challenge is to help the three youngest boys complete their educations. Education is so important. Maybe I can even learn to read and write. I would like that."

In 2005, mother, Geeta, and Chandra came to Florida to visit Ling and I. By now, Ling and her family were legal residents of the United States. Mike came from New York to see them.

We could tell this was going to be mother's last visit because she was slowing down, becoming forgetful, and needed someone with her all the time.

As usual she gave my husband lots of credit and mother thanked God he came into my life. She thought the world of him and his culture. She attended parties with us and enjoyed meeting my friends.

My mother and I went to a synagogue for a friend's daughter's Bat Mitzvah. There my mother prayed, whispering thanks to God for the former Jewish employers we'd had, and the income it provided for her sons' educations.

I wanted my mother to be proud of my home in Florida. I suggested we could walk on my dock, see the neighbor's boat, and watch folks jet ski in the river.

She observed, "You chose a very dangerous place to make your home. I can't swim and I don't know if you can. Living with a swimming pool, beside a river, and with a water retention pond are too risky for me and especially for children. What were you thinking?"

She added, "I can't understand why people pay so much money to live by water. It is so dangerous for the children and because of the hurricanes. Big bridges and fancy buildings don't fool me. I'm going back home to Trinidad to my village where I belong."

I shook my head at my sweet, humble mother, and realized there were no others like her in the universe.

Rajdaye Balkissoon in 2005. Mother of 11 children, step-mother of seven children, and grandmother of 50 children.

We all thank you. You taught us how to value independence and education, and 'Keep a still tongue and a wise head." You reminded us always to love, cherish and look out for each other, and we will.

Epilogue

In 1996, Ahmad and I, my children Mike and Kim, Ahmad's son BJ, and our daughter Jasmine returned to Florida as a family. Ahmad was working as an ER doctor. I continued to work as a nurse in geriatric care.

In 2008, I was a candidate for the Brevard County School Board District 3 because I believe in the value of public education, the appreciation of teachers, the importance of higher education and of vocational training.

I wanted people to know how much we struggled to get our education, and for people to value the educational opportunities here. I want to give people hope, motivation, and encouragement to improve their situation in life.

Considering the kinds of adversity I went through and I was able to move forward – If I could do it, anybody can.

My mother taught me the power of prayer and the importance of forgiveness.

This has made me a stronger, more confident person.

Fifty years later, Rajdaye still remembered fondly when she met Dhoon. "His car was an Austin Cambridge with license tag number PF2210!" No matter what, when mother talked about Dhoon, it was clear she really loved him.

Today Trinidad has evolved and society has change. Krishna and Rishi married Muslim girls, while Anand's wife is a Christian. Mike a/k/a Sunanda's first wife was Hindu and they had a boy and a girl. He married for the second time to an Italian Hare-Krishna woman and they had two sons. A nephew married a girl of mixed race: Indian-black-and Chinese. Our generation has made significant leaps that were once thought impossible.

In 2012, Rajdaye lives with Geeta in Trinidad and is surrounded by her loving children who contribute to her care. Her memory now is not what it used to be but she was able to contribute to this book.

❧ ❦ ❧

I am active in Democratic Party politics, member of American Business Women's Association (ABWA), Space Coast Progressive Alliance, Melbourne Chamber of Commerce, the Space Coast Writers' Guild (SCWG), and numerous women's groups, and the owner of small businesses. I wrote a column for our daily newspaper. I work in my chosen profession as a geriatic-care nurse. Without an education and a career, I would never have been able to create a life different from my mother's. I found my purpose in life and it is to use my life experience to help others.

My teenaged daughter and I went to Washington, D.C., to the Jon Stewart Restore Sanity Rally; and to a peace rally on the Mall. Several times, I've been a delegate to the Florida Democratic Conventions, and was chosen as a Hilary Clinton Delegate for Brevard County, Florida.

At Democratic Party events where Seeta was photographed with then-Senator Barack Obama who is now the President of the United States, and with President Bill Clinton, Vice-President Joe Biden, Senator Bill Nelson, Representative Alan Grayson, Jill Biden, a group of friends, candidate Alex Sink, and Democratic Party Chair - Representative Debbie Wasserman Schultz. The 2012 Calendar sales benefit a women's shelter.

Most of Rajdaye's children and grandchildren achieved higher education or a skilled trade. She calls her self "the root" of all of us. We love, honor, and cherish her.

My husband taught me the value of self-respect. Ahmad is a peaceful and loving man who sees God and good in everything. He is a dedicated medical doctor. He also enjoys birds, fish, his pet cat Lucy and the livestock on his hobby farm. He is my soulmate and complements me.

Kimberly, Michael, and BJ graduated from University of Central Florida (UCF) and our daughter Jasmine attends the University of Florida (UF). It was my dream for all our children to be college graduates!

Over time, Mr. Motorbike's work habits changed. He learned to take initiative and continued to work two jobs: one in an autobody shop and another as a night security guard. Mr. Motorbike got involved with Karate, and learned to manage his anger. He attends church regularly, and now volunteers to help youth with their self-control. He has been happily married for over 20 years. He has good relationships with all his children, including his daughter by his second marriage. Mr. Motorbike and his wife have become good friends with Ahmad and I.

Meeting Ahmad changed my life and the lives of my children in every good way possible. It is said, "God sends an angel when you most need it," and for me, this was true.

❧❧❧

Left: Seeta with then Florida Governor Jeb Bush in 2000.

Below: Kimberly with Reverend Al Sharpton and Representative Charles Rangel in the Atlanta International Airport in 2008.

Jasmine and Kimberly with their mother
Seeta in 2005 in Satellite Beach, Florida.

It was a blessing that I, as a girl from a small village, could have achieved so much through the power of positive thinking, prayer, education, good friends, my hardwork, and a strong marriage. I have a backbone of steel, a great family, and determination. I became a U.S. Citizen, and met two U.S. Presidents and one U.S. Vice President. Who would have predicted the little girl under the lemon tree would have gotten this far in life and be so bold?

I had the opportunity to emigrate from Trinidad to the U.S.A. By immigrating to the States, I paved the way for my siblings and opened their eyes to see that there is a life bigger than Ben Lomond village.

Believe in the power of your dreams, because anything is possible.

Our mother and father were able to instill in us that we must look out for each other, no matter what. I hope our children continue to do that also.

Seeta, Kimberly, Ahmad Sr., Ahmad Jr. "BJ", Jasmine, and Michael in Satellite Beach, Florida.

Seeta at WMEL-1300 am radio station.

As a little boy when Seeta would send me things, such as a pair of socks, most of the time, I was so in awe of getting it, I didn't want to use it. I couldn't conceive of pulling that sock on to walk across the floor, or putting it on a foot and sticking it inside the shoe. How could I do that to such a special gift? It was like a piece of jewelry! The socks were wrapped in a covering that read, "Made in the U.S.A."

We loved Seeta and missed her. All I wanted was to have my sister move back home. Although I cherished the gifts she sent, I longed for her to come back home. She couldn't, of course.

Seeta was the visionary, and she was the one who had embodied the idea that each of us could make a better life. She had that idea.

What would have happened if she had stayed in Trinidad? It's easy to look back now; with the benefit of hindsight, everything looks different.

In Hinduism, we say, "This is your karma." The law of karma is such – This was her destiny; This was where Seeta had to make her life. If she wasn't working in America, she couldn't have helped our mother. Seeta helping mother allowed mother to help me get an education and a law degree.

Anand Ramlogan
Attorney General
Trinidad & Tobago

Acknowledgments

Thank you my wonderful husband Ahmad Begui; to my parents Rajdaye and Dhoon; my 17 siblings: Chandra, Narine, Elsie "Dede," Toya, Curtis, Sugars, Rueben "Mascal," Latchman "Dreds," George (deceased), Sarah "Dolly," Molly, Sunanda "Mike," Geeta, Ling, Anand, Krishna, and Rishi; to my children Kimberly, Michael, Jasmine, and Ahmad Jr. "BJ"; to my nieces and nephews, cousins and all their children; and to all our extended families of Ramlogans and Balkissoons from the villages of Corial, Gasparillo, and Ben Lomond, Trinidad, I hope you enjoy this book and the memories you gave me.

Special thanks to all my friends for their encouragement, especially Julie Harrison, Laura Fausone, Eric, Jacque, Bonnie Katz, Shahla Shahsavari, Maxine, Tammy, Ginny, Marsha, Shantie, Rekha, Tatiana, Latta, Vindra, Bonnie, Esther, Denise, Nasreen Qazi, and my Not Quite MENSA Book Club members Christine, Cindy, Jane, Leslie, Susan, and former member, Ursula.

Thank you to Michael Everett for the bookcover design, and to Moji Thompson for the photograph of Corial which appears on the bookcover. Thank you to Linda Jump for the author photograph in the **About the Author** section on the last page.

Thank you to the following people who stood with me to see it through: Patricia A. McDonough for encouragement, friendship, believing in the project and in-depth copyediting; to Suzanne Witenhafer, R. Bradley Witenhafer and Katrina Thomas for help with the early drafts; and to Linda Jump, Ed von Koenigseck, Dr. Frances Rinaldi, and Andy Vazquez for copyediting, constructive criticism, and long hours of proofreading; to Keyon Jason Jordan for his personal knowledge of Trinidad and Tobago government, politics, geography, and the educational systems then and now.

About the Book

The book *Eighteen Brothers and Sisters, a memoir by Seeta Begui,* demonstrates how a mother's love imbued values and strength to her children, no matter their circumstance. Seeta's mother Rajdaye's wisdom emphasized obtaining an education. That value played out in the lives of her children, especially her daughter Seeta.

Two beautiful women, both trendsetters breaking traditions, are also stubborn and intelligent. The choices they make in life take them on an adventure. However, with no formal education, Rajdaye herself believed her children must become educated to find good jobs to have better lives. She was equipped with common sense and determination, she struggled to survive with many children by three men and challenges in a culture of arranged marriage.

Her daughter Seeta sets out to change the world, but with limited education, she emptied bedpans and cleaned toilets to work her way out of an abusive marriage, get an education and catapult herself into a better life.

Both women suffered at the hands of men. Seeta and Rajdaye had unconventional lives, with ambition as a driving force.

Surprisingly, an arranged marriage aided in helping Seeta to escape. The pathway for Seeta's future changed when she met a woman who taught her to believe in herself, make a life plan, and find a profession that was in demand. This changed her life forever. She empowered herself by immigrating to the U.S.A., becoming a nurse, and created her own world of compassion, political activism, public service, and family values.

How to Order This Book

Seeta is available for speaking engagements, book talks, and also workshops on subjects such as escaping domestic violence, empowerment of women, and the need for education and training.

Eighteen Brothers and Sisters by Seeta Begui may be purchased from the Webstore at www.seetamedia.com, by email to seetamedia@aol.com, or 321-271-6740 between 9 A.M. and 4 P.M., or from amazon at www.amazon.com/Eighteen-Brothers-Sisters-Seeta-Begui, where the eBook is also available.

Call us for information about quantity orders of the book to be used as fund raisers for a nonprofit groups.

About the Author Seeta Begui

Seeta Begui is a Licensed Practical Nurse happily married, living with her husband an Emergency Medicine Physician in Satellite Beach, Florida. She is the proud mother of four grown children.

She is active in Democratic Party politics, member of American Business Women's Association (ABWA), Space Coast Progressive Alliance, Melbourne Chamber of Commerce, the Space Coast Writers' Guild (SCWG), and numerous women's groups, and the owner of small businesses. I wrote a column for our daily newspaper. I work in my chosen profession as a geriatic-care nurse. Without an education and a career, I would never have been able to create a life different from my mother's.

Seeta promotes social justice, prevention of domestic abuse, education, and the empowerment of women. She wrote a column for the Gannett newspaper, *FLORIDA TODAY*. She is the host of "Viewpoints with Seeta" on WMEL 1300 am radio. "I found my purpose in life and it is to use my life experience to help others. I'm proud to be one of 18 children."